ReDiscover Dating

What's Keeping You from Getting Back Out There?

How to connect, gain confidence, and find love again

Larry W. Stone

SMG

Stone Media Group

This book details the author's personal experiences and opinions. The author is not a healthcare provider. The content herein is therefore not intended to be a substitute for professional medical advice, diagnosis, treatment or cure of any condition. Always seek the advice of a physician and/or other qualified mental health professional regarding any medical/psychological concerns. Although the author and publisher have made every effort to ensure that the information in this book was correct at press time, the author and publisher do not assume and hereby disclaim any liability to any party for any loss, damage, or disruption caused by errors or omissions, whether such errors or omissions result from negligence, accident, or any other cause. You are responsible for your own choices, actions, and results. The author and publisher are providing the book and its contents for entertainment purposes only. The experiences are real, however, some names and identifying details have been changed to protect the privacy of individuals.

ISBN 978-1-7331546-0-4

Stone Media Group

Fredericksburg, Virginia

Cover Design: Jody Bamber

Editing: Alpha Consulting

DEDICATION

This book is dedicated to Aurora & Liam, the first of many beautiful grandchildren. The two of you light up our world. Cynde & I are truly blessed to have you. Every moment we share with you is a reminder of how good God is.

CONTENTS

ACKNOWLEDGMENTS

I am thankful for so many…

Thank you to my beautiful wife Cynde, for your unending love and support. Everyone that knows you is blessed by your kind, nurturing spirit. Once we met, this book's rough draft may have sat forever unfinished. It was your encouragement that helped me to see it to completion.

Special thanks my parents, Jesse & Peggy Stone, along with my siblings, Debbie, Brenda & Russell for believing in me when I had the silly idea to write a book about dating while I was still dating (and not always doing such a good job of it). Your support has meant so much.

Thank you to our family; to Jody, thank you for all your years of unending, loyal support and behind the scenes effort. I have learned so much from your patience and wisdom over the years.

To Ryan, thank you for the years of tech support, and pushing me kicking and screaming into the 21st century. I may have given up many times without your help.

To Bri & Serena, thank you for the joy of giving me a hard time, of laughter, and for sharing your Mom with me.

To my mother in-law Dixie for laughter, and all the hot meals when I was starving (which was most of the time).

I want to thank Brandi Merryman for all the work you've done behind the scenes to make this project possible.

Thank you to the Fontana family for letting me share Michael's story. Michael, you will live on in my heart forever. Those who knew you still marvel at your way of seeing the world. Any time I have a bad day, you are my example to how I can choose to see it in a different light.

Thank you to my editor, Alpha Consulting for your uplifting encouragement.

Special thanks to Cynde Stone, Patti Huppmann, Charlene Snyder,

Michele Griffin, Jackie Otto, Christian Lane, Jason Iannicelli, Jody Bamber, Brenda Powenski, Jay Jackson, Chris Keyser and Carolyn Christiansen for your wise and constructive input throughout.

Special thanks to Linda Strand; without that first blind-date you set me up on, I might still be single, sitting home eating Cheetos and watching football with my dog Copper.

Much gratitude also to a few friends I've never met...Pat Flynn, Joanna Penn, Kirsten Oliphant, Tim Grahl, Dave Chesson and Chandler Bolt. These podcasters have been my daily dose of inspiration to see this book to completion.

Thank you to God, for providing me with this loving family support that I certainly don't deserve.

INTRODUCTION

"You are never too old to set another goal, or to dream a new dream." - C.S. Lewis

We arranged to meet at the Hyperion, a coffee shop in my hometown of Fredericksburg, Virginia. I had discovered her on the dating site OkCupid. Her profile lacked any photos, and she had written only a brief description of herself. I was struck though by our results of a 99 percent personality match, based on questions we had each previously answered on the site.

While her lack of profile photos would normally have turned me away, our personality match intrigued me enough to reach out. After many text and email conversations over several days, we arranged a meeting. Little did I know this would be the culmination of the long journey I had set out on.

I waited outside the entrance, watching for a lady named Cynde that I had only seen a single picture of. I remember well the excitement when our eyes met from across the street. Sitting that evening in the coffee shop, I hung on her words. I was drawn to her stories as she told me about herself. The person she was describing rang in my ear as the person I had been searching for. The air-conditioning vent at my feet had frozen me solid, but I didn't dare move away from our conversation.

She shared with me sometime later that she was sure I would never want to see her again, given all the boring stories she had told me. But I had felt just the opposite. That night I called my mom and told her that somehow, I knew I had met the one.

I found out later that she had no intentions of meeting me that day yet hadn't found a respectable way to cancel. In fact, she was only online at the urging of a co-worker who had told her she shouldn't remain single the rest of her life.

I often think of how different my life would be today if I hadn't reached out to her faceless profile on that dating site, or if she had cancelled and we had never met.

We met at the same location several more times. Each time I found myself drawn to this person with the kind, thoughtful eyes. Something was very different about this person than all the other outstanding people I'd met in my quest to find love.

As I write this, I am drawn to her as much today as the first day we met. We think alike, are both easygoing, and have the same goals and ambitions. This makes life together smooth and sweet. Over the years we continue to grow closer, and I am constantly amazed at how well our personalities fit together.

This was the relationship that I had set out for, and I had not found her by accident. I want to share with you how a naturally shy person with little confidence in himself got to this wonderful place that I am now, and how you can make use of the same game plan to build the relationship that you want. I thank God every day for allowing me to meet my wife, and I know there are plenty of single people who would benefit from what I've learned along the way. I spent years learning what I can teach you in a few short hours.

The world of technology constantly offers new tools for dating from websites to apps and social media. These tools will evolve as technology changes, but the ability to connect with other people lies firmly grounded in you. This book focuses on who you are and how you interact more than the tools themselves.

Your personality, and the way you show it to the world will ultimately be the best tool in your arsenal. While the technology you use to distribute that information will change, your ability to connect to another person once you are face-to-face will not.

For Those Fighting Anxiety or Depression

Each one of us is different, and approaches love and dating with a unique perspective and background. I had a great childhood and grew up in a stable home. Your life experiences may have differed from mine, and therefore your hurdles may be greater. I don't minimize that in any way. We never know what another person has been through if we haven't walked in their shoes.

While one person may have only minor issues with confidence and getting back out there, another may feel overcome with anxiety. Regardless,

I feel this course gives you the most direct route to take yourself from where you are now to a more confident, outgoing you.

I am not a trained professional, but I have a lot of real-world experience helping family members, friends, and coworkers who have suffered with anxiety. This has given me a unique perspective into the thought processes that can keep sufferers from moving forward, even when it's the best thing for them. While this book isn't just for those suffering with anxiety, it is laid out in a way that will help those of you that are.

If you fight depression, you are not alone. Many people quietly struggle with depression and anxiety but too few seek help. I truly believe everyone can benefit from the tips, techniques, and strategies put forth in this book.

If, however, you are hoping to find someone to make you happy, or you struggle regularly with depression, I urge you to talk to your pastor or mental health professional for help. The life you change could be your own.

The Basics

I designed this book to get you back out into a world of wonderful opportunities, while helping you achieve the dating confidence you desire. It will give you the avenues to meet more people and point you in the right direction to find a partner that will enrich your life.

It is designed to lead you through individual, actionable steps, each step leading you to greater confidence in yourself. In writing this, I looked at the individual steps taken in my journey from an incredibly shy teenager to the happy, confident person that I am today. I coupled those with the steps I took to gain a social life after becoming single again. Ultimately, this odyssey led me to meet the love of my life and have a relationship that is both strong and fulfilling.

This book covers eight main topics. They are:

1) Mindset

What is your thought process and perspective as you step back into the dating world? Mindset plays a major role throughout your entire dating experience.

2) What's Special About Me?

Finding and recalling the special traits you bring to the world.

3) Who Am I Looking For?

What are the character traits of the person who would fit well with your personality and lifestyle?

4) Dating Safety

Planning ahead for things you may not have considered regarding online and in-person safety.

5) Matchmaking and the Digital Connection

This section discusses connecting with other singles through friends and dating apps. These are often the easiest ways to get started, because you can initiate it before you physically step foot back out there.

6) Stepping Back Out into a Social World

Here we discuss putting yourself in a position to meet new people, make new friends, and create a social network for dating through Meetup groups. This section will also include important topics such as rejection and approach anxiety.

7) Everyday Connections

This segment builds upon the steps you learned in earlier sections to give you confidence in everyday life to meet single people all around you.

8) Dating

This final section takes you from first meeting to becoming exclusive, with questions to ask yourself along the way to stay on track toward the goal of meeting the right person.

Here are just a few of the things that we will also cover on your journey:

- Finding what really matters to you in another person.
- Recognizing what your strengths are.
- Recognizing what goes on in your head that keeps you from meeting others.
- Learning how to change routines to discover new people and possibilities.
- Learning great ways to meet people.
- Releasing shyness one step at a time.
- Building your confidence by doing new things.
- Gaining a new perspective on dating possibilities.
- Seeing things from a broader perspective.
- Expanding your social network.

- Meeting the type of person you are looking for.

Let's take this journey together, and I know you will surprise yourself in what you are capable of. It is not based on how good looking you are, how much money you make, or how intelligent you are. The difference will be made in the decision to move forward with your life today, following the strategies that make up your game plan, connecting with others outside your current circle, and building confidence in small, achievable steps.

When you commit to this book and explore all the ways to expand your social world, you will find that you have incredible options awaiting you. The sky is the limit. Allow yourself to experience these challenges, and you just may find that special someone just around the corner.

CHAPTER 1
STARTING OVER

"The size of your dreams must always exceed your current capacity to achieve them. If your dreams do not scare you, they are not big enough." - Ellen Johnson Sirleaf

"Where do I even begin?" I asked myself. I had been divorced 1,827 days. I hadn't gone on a date of any sort since Ronald Reagan was president. My social connections had dried up long ago, and outside of work, I spent my free time with my two kids.

I was sure that I would get turned down by anyone I asked out and had no clue who I might consider asking out anyway. One thing I knew for sure though; I didn't want to end up in anything short of a great relationship. That fear, however, also kept me from trying anything at all.

So, I spent all my spare time with my kids, our dog Copper, and our cat, Alley. This created a cocoon of safety which protected me from having to meet new people and get involved in anything that might take me out of my comfort zone. My natural shyness and lack of confidence had me pinned to the floor, and I hadn't even considered wrestling with it.

I needed to find a way out of the routine that was providing me safe refuge from meeting others in the real world. As I began hunting for ways to get out of my own safe zone, I wondered if I was the only one struggling with this.

Later, as I got back out into the singles scene, I began to meet others that were having the same struggles, and for those that were shy, the struggle was the toughest. I began taking meticulous notes and decided then that I would share what I learned about what did and didn't work with the rest of the world. In doing so, I hope I can help others on the same quest.

If you have been through a breakup in the last year, it is important to take the proper time to heal before putting yourself in an emotionally charged expedition. It is far too easy to fall into the next relationship before healing completely from the last. Rebound relationships nearly always lead to disaster. Once you have healed, you will find this book will help you start again.

Each one of us is different. You may be naturally outgoing but have lost connection with any semblance of a social life. You may lack self-confidence and can't see how that body you see staring back in the mirror could ever be attractive to another. You may naturally be shy and have never had a social outlet to begin with. At different times in my life, I felt I had been all three.

The steps laid out in this book offer you tools to better understand your apprehension, build confidence, and create new habits that will make you a more dynamic person. This is the book I wish I'd been able to find when I started. I've been on this journey, and I know what finding the right person has meant to my life. Stick with me and let this process carry you on the same path.

CHAPTER 2
MY JOURNEY

"If you do what you've always done, you'll get what you always got." - Tony Robbins

Growing up, I was the shyest person you could have ever met. I never talked to anyone outside of close friends. My shyness seemed to have started when I was in the first grade. My Aunt Edna was visiting from Florida, and my mom was handing out my school photo. She exclaimed with a laugh "Look at those ears!" It was the first time I can remember even being aware of myself, and what I looked like.

That single statement started the wheels turning in my head that somehow, I was different. I recall running to the bathroom mirror to take a look. I can laugh about the comment now, but it immediately made me conscious of my ears, and I became hypersensitive that I was different. If you looked at my school photos in the years following, you would see that I began growing my hair longer to cover those appendages. It wasn't until I was 33 years old that I had the nerve to cut it short and expose my ears to sunlight again.

As I entered middle school, I earned the nickname "Bones." I was small and scrawny. I never wanted to "stand out" in a crowd and would take any opportunity to disappear from the rest of the world.

As I got older, I didn't grow much. I was the kid who weighed 79 pounds going into high school, 15 pounds of which was acne, and another 10 pounds of ears. I've been reminded of my shyness many times over the years when I've run into old classmates who did not recall me by face or by name, even though I'd been in the same class with them for multiple years. They simply had no recollection of me.

When I got my first job out of high school, my life started to change. I became interested in fitness as a way to add a few pounds to my tiny physique, and took a job at our local YMCA, eventually working my way up to a fitness instructor. Without even being aware of the evolution, I was gaining confidence, and breaking out of my shyness. Being more physically fit and having people come to me for advice started to break down the shyness barrier that had kept me caged up in my own head for so long. This helped me to quell a bit of my poor self-image. Working in a public situation, and teaching others stretched my comfort zone, and helped me build my confidence.

During this same time, my love of music began to test my shyness even further. I put myself out in the public eye through music. I formed a band with a friend. I had seen my confidence go up, and I wondered if I could overcome my fear of performing in front of people. This was my first foray into purposely making myself vulnerable to criticism from the outside world.

Trust me when I say there is a reason that I am not in the music business. I gave it 100 percent effort, but that did not mean I always did it well. Looking back, the experience helped me grow in ways I would never have imagined.

One tip that I picked up from others during this time was that everyone experiences butterflies in their stomach, whether or not we are shy. That was a big surprise to me. I always assumed I was the only one! I also recognized that while some people shutter at the thought of performing live, others revel in it. What one person refers to as panic, another describes as excitement jitters. I mention this because it happens in all walks of life, and this happens in the dating world. How we perceive what we are about to do often plays a more important role than the actual event. Each time I conquered a step, my fear would dissipate a bit, as my comfort level grew.

I also observed that the more I worried about how I would play on stage, the worse I did. The more practice I got in, the higher my confidence and comfort level grew. The more regularly that our band played in public, the more I got out of my own head, and could immerse myself in the music. Place those three observations on any dating situation, and you see that they will fit there as well.

I discovered a positive demeanor and a smile are attractive to others, and I gained many friends, and truly began to enjoy being in a much bigger world of possibilities than I could have ever imagined.

I have always loved to learn, and I so I began reading books on confidence and other related topics, searching for tools that would help me grow outside my little world. As I did, I realized the techniques these books taught were often things that I had already done on my own. I noted how they were not weird psychobabble, but ways for people who didn't naturally have these skills to learn and make use of them, just as a person can take dance or music lessons.

Over the next twenty years I continued to expand my comfort zone, trying many things I would have naturally refrained from doing before. This included public speaking, singing in public, and becoming the president of a small company, which often meant working with large groups of people. I was changing from an incredibly shy person to being comfortable with myself in social situations.

During my married years, much of my social network eroded away, as family needs replaced the time once reserved for friends and fun. This is an expected change for most of us as life priorities shift.

Unexpected Change

Over the years, it became clear that my wife and I wouldn't stay married. The resulting separation and divorce brought lots of life changes, an underlying depression, and a renewal of all the questions I used to ask myself. For several years after our split, my kids and my business kept life very busy. I stayed too busy to consider the thought of finding someone new. I was confident in who I was as a businessperson, but terrified of "putting myself back out there."

I hadn't been on a date, much less a social gathering as a single person since George Lucas had written Star Wars: The Empire Strikes Back. Apart from church, I did not belong to any other social circles. By the time I realized I really wanted to get back out there and meet someone, years had passed, and any confidence that I once had was gone.

The last time that I'd dated there was no such thing as online dating, social media, or cell phones. The world had certainly changed a lot in those twenty-plus years.

Friends would give me unsolicited advice like "You'd better get back out there before you get too set in your single ways" or the ever optimistic, "Good luck finding anyone around here worth dating." There were those who seemed hopeful regardless of reality who told me, "She'll pop right into your life when you aren't looking for her." I was hoping for that last one to come true.

I liked the idea that this special someone would pop into my life when I least expected it. One of those late nights, the doorbell was going to ring, and a gorgeous single pizza delivery woman (aged 46) would be standing there. Of course, she would have had to throw herself at me, announce her singleness and interest, or nothing would have happened still.

Though I was confident in my work, I was clueless on how to get started when it came to finding a love relationship. I knew I didn't want to end up in some smoky bar searching for a partner, so hoping one would show up at the door with pizza was the best shot I thought had. It was a lonely time, full of insecurities swirling in my head, wondering if it would even be possible to find a great relationship.

Though I was scared to death, I knew I had to do it. I would get off the couch and find a way to meet other people. This is where it began to get uncomfortable, but somehow, I knew it would all be worth it.

I Was Ready

I searched online and in books for great ways to get back into the social scene after years away from it all. Most of the information I found for meeting women was full of bravado and hype. There was a lot of information out there about taking a woman home for the night. It felt sleazy and disingenuous.

I knew I wasn't the only one who wanted to find a lasting relationship. I determined to figure out how to do this myself. I began to approach it like a research project. This gave me the drive to go forward and to document what I tried, and why it worked or did not.

I decided that I would share my discoveries with the rest of the world when I did. I was writing the entire time I was dating. This research project was fun at times. At other times, it was trying. There were plenty of disheartening moments. However, I knew that ultimately this journey would lead me to a great relationship if I stuck with it, and I was right. Now I want to help you find someone special to create a great life with as well.

To help you focus on the action steps in this book, I've created the Rediscover Dating companion course. This guide will assist you in taking action and staying on top of your game plan throughout the book. This is your first step toward creating success in the journey. Download your free copy at www.RediscoverDating.com/course.

CHAPTER 3
MY MIND'S ROLE

"We cannot solve our problems with the same thinking that created them."
- Albert Einstein

We all know someone who can walk into a room and light it up. That was never me. I would enter a room, and no one would know I was even there. Confidence was that elusive X-factor that I had always wanted, but with no idea how or if I could attain it.

The ability to have confidence is something that any of us can attain. It is a change of perspective, brought on by taking action, and thus gaining competence. This competence puts your mind at ease, allowing you to be in the moment, and outside of your own head. You will notice the difference confidence makes in your thoughts, as well as your social and business life, as you grow beyond your comfort zone.

To make the most of this journey to find love, you need to consider that what's keeping you from finding someone isn't that there aren't any good people out there. You should consider the possibility that what's actually stopping you is what you believe about yourself.

For some of us, shyness is an added factor. When I was unsure of myself in a social situation, I wanted to fade into the background or disappear altogether. Since I kept to myself, few people noticed me. I did not talk to anyone, and no one talked to me. Many people never even realized I was there. Does that sound familiar?

What amazes me though, is that I often find some of the most fantastic, likable, and thoughtful people in that unconfident crowd. The problem lies in that most people do not know they exist as shy people have a natural tendency to want to fade into the wallpaper.

If you want to unlock your shyness, and let the world see you in a new light, I'll show you how I did it. I want to clarify that I am not trying to change who you are as a person. If you are looking to step beyond shyness and lack of confidence, I'll show you what worked for me. I know it can work for you as well.

Take one step at a time and continue reminding yourself that these small steps will change your perspective, your confidence, and your world. This world is looking for genuine, caring, and thoughtful people. It's time to let me introduce you to the rest of the world.

Am I Just Talking to Myself?

Each of us has developed a standard set of dialogue questions and answers in our own head that direct the way we see ourselves, our relationships, and the world around us. As I go through my day, I am talking silently to myself. This dialogue shapes my perspective of myself and the world around me. That inner conversation subtly governs my daily path and the decisions I make, just to name a few. The fact that I talk to myself isn't inherently good or bad. It does, however direct my thoughts, my behavior, and ultimately my life.

The conversations you have with yourself have evolved over a lifetime. They have either put you in a place of confidence or kept you from it. Your inner dialogue may have put you in a position to meet new people or may have helped you erect walls that keep you from it. Most of the time you don't even realize the conversation is going on, and how what's being said in your own head affects your decision making.

There are specific thought and life patterns that confident people have created, often without planning it, that give them their confidence. In the same way, there are specific patterns that cultivate a lack of confidence, which can leave you frustrated, shy, depressed, anxious, or pessimistic about your dating life.

So much of what keeps us from taking on the challenge and finding the right person lies between our ears. If we begin to see the roadblocks that we set up for ourselves, we can then deconstruct them.

That Can Change Take the time to follow through on these steps and get back out there. The life you change will be your own.

I'm happy to say that the patterns we develop at a young age can evolve. I am living proof of it. Fortunately, the evolution won't require you a lifetime of remolding either. This is something that you can begin reworking now and begin to see a real difference in a short period of time.

You Must Take Action to Make a Change

Before we begin, you must recognize that knowledge itself won't change your behavior. I'm guilty of getting excited about a book but failing to apply what I learned. I would end up with a short summary of the book in my head, without any actionable knowledge. Unless my habits change, I have gained nothing.

I've consolidated the steps it took for me to recreate my social life, grow my confidence, and find the love of my life in a disconnected world. This journey took me three years of slow discovery. I've distilled this knowledge into a step-by-step method that you can implement in a short time at your own pace.

CHAPTER 4
WHO AM I LOOKING FOR?

"Success is getting what you want. Happiness is liking what you get."
- H. Jackson Brown, Jr.

I bet it's both exciting and scary to think of a more confident you getting back out in the world and meeting new people. Let's take the first step by considering just who it is you want to meet. If you wanted to build a house, you wouldn't go out and start nailing two by fours together. Yet I often see single people searching with no plan for the kind of person they are looking for, or the relationship that they ultimately want to build.

We human beings are an interesting bunch. We like to think we are logical, rational decision-makers. But much of our decision making is based on emotion and subconscious thought processes. Once we've made that decision, we use logic to justify the rationality of our choices. It's that way whether you are buying a soda or finding a date.

You may say, "That's not me," but science says otherwise. It is helpful to know that emotion influences your decision-making more than you realize. So, my goal here is to dig deep on who and what you are looking for before you begin connecting with people.

As you read this, you can consider these things rationally. When you meet someone new, it is easy to get swept up in the moment, and some of that rationality can fly out of the window.

Have you considered in-depth the person you want to meet? This is the first and foundational building block to a great future. I spent a lot of time on this section in the initial stages of my planning. I wanted to get it right this time, and looking back, I'm so glad I did.

For me, outside of my Must-Haves (which we will discuss shortly), I was interested in finding someone that I enjoyed spending my time with. In a real sense, I was going to seek out a deep friendship with a person who I could also see myself having a romantic relationship with.

I realize this goes against every romantic scene at the movies where two people fall in love. At that point in my life, however, I realized that I wanted a partner that I would enjoy spending all my time with, not just the romantic moments. This was my starting search criteria. I began by looking at the circle of people I call my true friends, to see what traits had kept our friendships strong over the years.

If you are ready to skip this section, or skim read it, let me remind you that statistically, second marriages have an even higher divorce rate than first marriages, and third marriages have a sky-high divorce rate. What you learn here can help you choose the right relationship to begin with.

Friendships

Look at the long-term friendships you have. I'm speaking of those closest friends that you truly enjoy spending time with. There are reasons you enjoy spending time with that other person. If you two get along well, and enjoy one another's company, then you likely see the world from a similar viewpoint.

While I agree that you aren't just searching for a new best friend, I was looking for someone to love who could also be my best friend. I know the old saying "opposites attract." It might be fun and exciting at first, but you can grow to hate those differences once the honeymoon phase is over. Like-mindedness is the glue that will help hold a relationship together, in good times and in bad.

Consider what traits your best friend has that make you want to spend time together. There are some characteristics there that will clue you in on the type of person you enjoy being around. Don't overlook these in your future love life.

Past Relationships

Look at your past relationships. What traits did you find endearing? What characteristics warmed your heart. Was she always kind to animals? Did he think of others before himself? You may say "I like a guy in uniform" or "I want a lady who is size 8 or smaller." While these things may be a plus for you, none of them will create a happy relationship. They are only things that will please you for the moment.

Others Who Have Lived It

Consider other couples around you, the closer to you the better. What can you glean from those couples that have strong, loving relationships around you?

Your "Must-Haves"

What traits and characteristics are absolute necessities to you in any future relationship? It is far better for you to determine these traits now, before real human beings start populating your dating world. Without knowledge of the traits and characteristics you want in another person, it is easy to get swept up by looks, the appearance of a lavish lifestyle, or any number of other things.

What are Your "Must-Haves" in a Relationship?

Use the accompanying ReDiscover Dating Course to create your Must-Have's list. Go to www.ReDiscoverDating.com/course.

Your "Deal-Breakers"

Deal-Breakers are often easier to identify than your Must-Haves. You may have seen these traits in past relationships, and you want to avoid someone with these characteristics at all costs in the future. Hopefully, you are able to spot these traits from a mile away, but in the presence of a good-looking person, you can easily overlook these negatives.

Past Relationships

What negatives have you experienced in past relationships? What negatives have you seen resurface in multiple relationships of your own? Do you seem to find the "wrong" type of partner time and again? Have you found yourself trying to "save" other people from an addiction again and again? Have you been caught up in an abusive relationship, only to get out, and find yourself in another?

What are Your Deal-Breakers?

Be sure to compile your list of Deal-Breakers in the Companion course.

List out what you won't allow yourself to encounter in future relationships, beginning with any negative situations that you have repeatedly found yourself in. You must stay deeply focused on not stepping back into negative scenarios that you have been caught in before. Keep this list along with your Must-Haves in a place you can refer to them such as your phone or device, or at least on paper where you can readily refer to them.

Give both your Must-Have's and Deal-Breaker's list to a friend or mentor that you can trust to tell you what you need to hear, if you get off track. You will probably need to refer to these many times, so keep them available. We will discuss finding a coach in-depth in Chapter 10: Getting Help.

When you are meeting new people, it's easy to forget some of these things you've noted when swayed by a charming personality, or a stunning figure. This step is especially helpful if you have a habit of finding the wrong relationships in the past. Referring back to this list can help keep you on course.

Physical Attraction

You may have noticed there weren't any notations in this chapter regarding the physical features of the potential partner you are preparing to meet. It's not that physical features do not play a role in searching for the right partner. We all have physical characteristics that are attractive to us. There are three reasons I haven't noted them here.

1) Physical features are worn on the surface. You know what is and isn't physically attractive to you. You can easily see these features without having to dig deeper into who they are or list them.
2) Physical features only play a small role in long-term happiness, and many would say that it plays no long-term role at all.
3) I've heard many times people speak of how they could never date a guy who wore "such & such." While I can understand lack of knowledge in what to wear (just ask my wife), these aren't character traits, and for those of us who seem stuck in the "what not to wear" department, many will be open to accept some help. This shouldn't be a do or die scenario and can easily be overcome in many cases. Think about it. If you limit your choices based on dressing and appearances, you may turn your head away from the perfect match that meets other important characteristics. Just something to keep in mind.

What Does a Great Future Look Like?

Let's imagine that five years from today you run into an old friend from high school. The two of you stop for coffee to catch up. You tell your friend you've met and married your soulmate. The friend asks "So, how are things for you?" You reply, "Things have never been better." Take some time to describe in your companion course what made you give such a raving review of your life together. How does your partner treat you? How does your partner treat your family? What do you spend time doing together? How is life better than it was before you met?

As we wrap this chapter up, the following questions will help in the search. What kind of person will allow you to:

- Fulfill each other's dreams?
- Be there for each other's children?
- Motivate one another to grow to the next level?
- Make each of you a better person?
- Help you grow spiritually?
- Enjoy spending your time together every day?

With the right person, it's so much easier and more enjoyable to grow to your highest potential.

CHAPTER 5
FEELING GOOD ABOUT YOU

"Acceptance doesn't mean resignation; it means understanding that something is what it is and that there's got to be a way through it." - Michael J. Fox

Did you ever hear "You aren't smart enough" or "You aren't pretty enough?" Maybe growing up you heard "You can never do that" or "You are too big, or too small." In your own way, you may have heard some version of "Not good enough." Even if you never heard it, advertising, television, and the movies have constantly barraged you with the "perfect" look. With it, your self-esteem took a direct hit.

Making Comparisons

Whether it's your attractiveness, the size of your house, your waistline, or your bank account, you will compare yourself at times to the world around you. It's human nature. Being a photographer for close to three decades has put me in touch with many physically attractive people. I can say definitively that they are just as insecure as anyone else. I would bet that if you took a survey of the biggest names in Hollywood, you would find them just as concerned about their level of attractiveness as you. These are the pretty people that we think have it all!

Even after stating all that, I am sure that you don't feel any better about the things you dislike about yourself. At least you are in good company with the rest of us. Nearly all of us would like to be thinner, have more money, and be more confident.

Social media further plays its role by allowing us to see glimpses of other people's "perfect world," which is never actually as perfect as it may appear. It's far too easy to overlook the great things we have in our own lives when we compare ourselves to others. While the grass may look greener on the other side, it is just as often concealing problems underneath.

I believe in a God who loves me. Psalm 139:14 says "I am fearfully and wonderfully made". God did not make a mistake in creating me. Yet I am still so painfully aware of my own shortcomings.

Feeling Fit

These days more than ever, the demands of your everyday life can stop you from doing things that make you feel good about yourself. Whether it is your commute, the pressure of being a single parent, long workdays or other factors, it is easy to let your physical health get pushed aside. When you do, your confidence takes a hit.

It is essential to engage in physical activities to keep you feeling alive and reduce stress. These activities increase blood flow, produce positive changes to your brain, and lower the risk of death from common diseases. Exercise also makes you feel better about yourself, which contributes to your overall happiness.

Tracking Your Intake and Activity

If you struggle at all with weight and are looking for that first step, I'll suggest what I did. Download a calorie app and begin tracking your calorie intake for two weeks. Even if you do nothing else at first, that's usually an eye-opener. With technology, it is easier than ever to track. Your phone can easily track your activity as well. For most of us, a little less intake, and a little more exercise is a great place to start.

Small Changes Make a big Difference

It is easy to sit here and commit to a monumental change in routine. Instead of taking on a huge goal of planning to workout seven days a week for two hours a day, and then quitting by day three because the goal is too large and unsustainable, just start with three days a week of walking around the block. Once you get in the habit, extend that challenge and increase your level of activity.

Start first by planning time into your schedule, so you have a set time to do it. The hardest part is getting started. Get started anyway and don't beat yourself up if you miss a day. I personally feel like I'm always getting started. It's better to be getting to it 75 percent of the times you schedule your workout than to give up because you missed two days in a row. Just pick back up and get going again. Beating yourself up is self-defeating. Get back on your schedule and get moving. I know from my own experience that you feel better about yourself when you are exercising, even before you ever see any changes.

Activities

Take some time now to list some activities that you would enjoy. Examples include playing sports, working out, going dancing, joining an exercise class, or walking through the neighborhood three times a week.

If you aren't confident in how you look, don't wait until tomorrow to start. Put down this book and take the first step to improve it now. What can you do immediately to impact this area of your life? Reading alone won't make it happen. Meet this small challenge head on today!

Writing it down just brings it to awareness, but taking action makes the difference. Even minimal changes can boost your confidence in yourself. Don't wait until tomorrow to start.

Maybe you are thinking, "I'll just wait a while to start this dating thing until I've lost a few pounds." To which I say, "No way!" Let's get this train rolling now, right where you are at today. If we put off starting until things are perfect, there will always be something to keep you from moving forward. The journey begins today!

Appearance

If you need braces or dental work to improve your smile, set the date for a consultation and stop putting it off another day. I did that just as I began dating at the age of forty-five. I had been self-conscious of my smile since I was a kid. I really did not have the extra money in the budget to do so. However, I decided to go to two free consultations and explain my situation. Both offered a payment plan and the orthodontist I chose offered other suggestions to lower costs that I would not have expected.

It made all the difference in my confidence with the opposite sex. It literally allowed my brain to stop wondering constantly what my date was thinking about my teeth. I would do it all over again in a heartbeat and often wonder what took me so long.

Acceptance

You might worry about things you cannot easily change. This could be the shape of your face, how large your nose is, how big your ears are, and your height or body shape. I have literally been looking in the mirror since I was a kid, wondering if I could get my ears pinned back, so I did not look like a taxicab with its doors open. Like it or not, the things you can't easily change make you unique.

Recognizing these traits and body differences for what they are and determining to change the way you talk to yourself about them, can help you see yourself as a worthy date. As you make changes to the things you can, your confidence level will increase naturally. As hard as it is for me to believe, the things that bothered me most about myself did not keep me from meeting my perfect partner.

What would have kept me from meeting her is if I had not gotten back out there in the real world because I was too worried about it. I encourage you to look around. There's plenty of proof everywhere you go that it's not just the best-looking people who find love!

I'm not saying looks don't count, but they are only one part of the equation of you. You don't see an accurate picture of yourself when you look in the mirror. Your areas of concern are often greatly exaggerated by your own beliefs and perspective. It is easy to place your sole focus on that, as if your other qualities don't count. But they do, and far more than you may realize. I've seen people of all shapes, sizes and challenges find love, and you can too.

What one thing can you change that would make the single most difference in your confidence level? If it is changeable, what is the first step to making it happen? What's stopping you from making that first step happen now? Can you schedule it by the end of today? If so, get started on it right away. Take action to make it happen.

If it is not changeable, what perspective shift do you need to make to accept it and move forward?

What's Holding You Back?

If you hesitate to get back out there because you are overweight, statistically; you are in good company. According to the Center for Disease Control and The National Institute of Health, one in three Americans is considered overweight, while another one in three individuals is considered obese. This means roughly two-thirds of Americans are above their ideal weight. If that is you, then you are not alone. Get out there anyway! If you aren't happy where you are, begin work on it today in little steps. Avoid letting this deter you from getting started though.

In my work on this book, many people told me they were concerned that their finances would make them a poor dating prospect to others. According to CNN, in 2018, 61 percent of Americans would be unable to pay for a $1,000.00 unplanned expense. Once again, you would be in good company. Just like an exercise plan, a budget plan to get out of debt shows others you are working through it. That is far more attractive than sitting on the couch worrying about it. My suggestion is to get a plan underway to change this but don't let it delay you in getting back out there. These are just a few examples of the many things people say would hold them back from dating. I say move forward anyway. It's time to tell yourself, "This is me. I'm going to accept that and move forward!"

CHAPTER 6
RECOGNIZE THE GREAT THINGS ABOUT YOU

"If you talked to your friends the way you talk to yourself, would you have any?"
- Anonymous

As we get started in this section, I want to tell you it is your time to shine. The world needs you and your unique gifts. I know in my heart that some of the most kind, caring and thoughtful people are naturally shy, quiet, or lack the confidence to give dating a real launch without a good push. I am here to help with that. God knows how important you are to this world. I'd be willing to bet you have family, friends, or coworkers who have been urging you to get back out there. Let's take time to look at the things that make you special.

Who are You?

- What do you enjoy most about life?
- What is important to you?
- What really gets you excited?

Let's take some time to work through this section. Be sure to fill these out in your free companion course, as they will give you good insight into yourself and who you are looking for. In addition, you will use what you write in upcoming sections. You can visit www.RediscoverDating.com/course to download that free copy of the accompanying course that I have created to help you stay on track.

Your Personal Positive Qualities List

What assets do you bring to the table? Make a list of twenty positive things about yourself. Consider all aspects of who you are. Name everything you can think of, no matter how small or obscure you think it is. They can be traits, positive things you see about yourself, character qualities, intellectual highlights, skills, accomplishments, natural talents, and things that you have overcome. If you get stuck, think of positive things others have complimented you on.

Use this list anytime that you need a boost, or for things to talk about when questioned on a date. There is a lot that is special about you. It's easy when you begin dating again to only focus on your weaknesses or negative traits and forget how many amazing things there are about you!

Recognize that God made you wonderfully unique. Make the most of who you are! Start by realizing it. Don't skip this step, as it will be very helpful in a future chapter!

Remember Your Past Accomplishments

Create a list in your companion course workbook of all the past accomplishments in your life. It is easy to stack up many accomplishments, but they tend to be forgotten. What are things that you have accomplished or overcome in your life? Name them, creating a list of at least fifteen. Do not be shy. If you made it happen, write it down. Examples here could include things like being the first in your family to get your bachelor's degree, learning to play guitar, overcoming your fear of singing in public, getting your GED, giving up smoking, and more. Do not worry about whether the achievement is worthy of making it on the list, or if it is worthy of an award or not. If it is an accomplishment, write it down.

Now, take all you've gathered so far from both lists, and fill this out as if you were writing a personal resume about yourself. It may help to look at the information that you have gathered and pretend to be writing for a friend. The good things you would say about someone else are sometimes hard to say about yourself.

We all have areas we want to improve on. Choose to accept where you are as your starting point. There is no reason to wait to get out there. It's time to let the world know about you!

CHAPTER 7
GET OUT OF YOUR OWN WAY!

"It doesn't matter where you came from, only where you are going."
- Brian Tracy

I realized that the day I stopped making excuses for why I couldn't do something, was the day I finally got to work on how I could. All of us have things we want to do in life, but never seem to get around to. I have always wanted to learn to play piano. But after owning a keyboard for over thirty years, I have only learned one song. It was just never a priority. That is ok. If it happens, it happens. It has just never really been important enough to make it to the top of the priority list.

Finding love, however, was incredibly important to me. I had been wanting to do that for a long time. Yet not knowing where to start, coupled with the fear of getting started, had kept me from trying. It took a change of perspective to get me moving.

That mind shift came on a July 4 outing to watch fireworks with my family. As the evening progressed, I realized that I was letting this part of my life slip by due to inaction. I was sick of not having someone to share life with.

It was at that moment that I determined I would no longer sit still and watch life go by without me. It was time to jump in headfirst, or face being alone the rest of my life. This was the moment where the desire to make it happen was larger than the fear that stopped me. That was my defining moment, the first of many to come.

Now I was finally ready. Being ready for a change was my biggest ally in reaching for my goal. Where are you? Are you ready to take the next step forward? Doing so will require effort and persistence, but most importantly, a willingness. Realize this is a new season and look forward to what is just around the corner!

Self-Esteem, Self-Confidence, and Shyness

I want to say again that I am not a psychologist or a doctor. I am just a guy who went through this process and kept my eyes open to the challenges and concerns other singles were having around me. My explanations are from my own viewpoint.

Often, shyness, self-esteem, and self-confidence are discussed interchangeably, as though they were all the same thing. While they are separate concepts, they are interrelated and often overlap one another. Let us take a closer look.

Self-Esteem

Self-esteem refers to how much value that you believe you have in the world, or how you feel about yourself overall as a person. A simple way to look at it is, it's how much positive regard you have for yourself.

Self-Confidence

Self-confidence refers to how assured you are of your abilities in any given situation. It is typically related to achievement, in one sense or another. Since it is situational, you can be very confident in your ability to play guitar yet scared to death to talk to people in a social setting.

Shyness

Being shy means, you have a general discomfort in social encounters, which is further heightened by being around people you are not familiar with. While most people feel shy at least on some occasions, you may have such an intense shyness that it affects your ability to interact even when you want to. Shy people are often overly self-conscious.

Many people experience issues with shyness, self-esteem and self-confidence together. Genetics, your life experiences, and the questions that you have asked yourself over the years have likely shaped your self-esteem and self-confidence, as well as any shyness.

Fortunately, all is not lost. None of these perceptions are permanently set and can be reshaped as you would a piece of clay, given some time. Since they are interrelated, working on one can improve the other. Stepping out of my comfort zone and looking for the little victories along the way has shown me that that it is not a permanent trap.

Confidence Comes from Doing

Experience has taught me it is possible to be completely confident in one aspect of your life while having zero confidence in another. I was confident in my work as a professional photographer but had no confidence in my ability to approach the opposite sex. Walking into a room full of new people would scare me to death. The only thing that got me past the fear practicing it. Each time I did it I became a little more comfortable.

You will enhance your confidence by attempting new things and gathering small achievements as you do. Your confidence naturally rises with your competency level.

Each step you take, from deciding to create a life change, stepping out from shyness, or reaching past your fear of rejection will make you stronger. The exciting part is that you are literally rewriting your future through each success.

You can find people in every walk of life who have risen above their negative situations and used them as a catalyst for change. The questions you ask yourself in any given situation, and how you decide to answer them will determine your outcome.

Starting from Scratch

The way to gain confidence is by stepping out of your comfort zone. It is how you acquire confidence in anything. The fear you feel as you step into anything new is perfectly normal, and everyone feels this at times. I always thought I was the only one with this experience. I've run into many others who thought similarly. This feeling typically has led them to keep it to themselves, not realizing that this experience is quite normal.

I first realized this when I set out to get over my lifelong fear of roller coasters. Our family had season passes to Kings Dominion, an amusement park in Doswell, Virginia. At the beginning of the season, my daughter Jody had exclaimed that she was not only going to get me on my first roller coaster, but she would get me on every coaster in the park that year. Half of me was thrilled at the idea of conquering this fear, and the other half was scared to death.

After dragging me onto the kid's rollercoaster, the Scooby Doo (sounds scary, doesn't it?), Jody began taking me to all the other rollercoasters in the park. Each one gave me an adrenaline rush, and a surge of confidence that I could move on toward the next. She was taking me through her own version of what therapists call exposure therapy. Exposure therapy does not just work by getting you used to experiencing the fear. It also re-trains your brain to stop sending signals of impending fear when you do not face any real danger.

We were now in line for a much larger coaster, the "Hypersonic XLC." According to Wikipedia, this was the first compressed air coaster in the world, with a top speed of eighty mph and a vertical drop.

As I stood there in line, I realized that other people in my group were also experiencing some degree of anxiety about this new blast coaster, which surprised me. They seemed to enjoy the adrenaline rush, feeling enthusiastic and excited by it. They were feeling the same anxiety that struck terror in me, but they were somehow enjoying the sensation.

Their perspective on the same event was so different from mine! They were seeking the very adrenaline rush that I wanted to run away from. It was then that I realized there that there was a difference in how each of us perceives a new situation with risk. How I perceived that feeling shaped the way I approached it; with fear or excitement.

Roller coasters aren't a high-risk activity. According to the International Association of Amusement Parks as reported by ABC News in 2013, the risk of getting killed on a coaster is one in 750 million. It is really not about risk, but more about the way I associated that activity in my mind, such as loss of control.

The roller coaster ride is the same every time. If we polled a group of people, we would find some that love roller coasters, and we would discover a group that said, "No way, not for me." It is not about safety. It really boils down to how we hold the thought of that activity in our mind.

What does this example have to do with dating? Everything! Some people love the idea of dating, meeting new people, and the excitement of new relationships. In all actuality, they probably are not reading this book. For those of us who dread the thought of getting back out there, the problem lies in how we hold the thought of dating in our mind. One person says that it is exciting and thrilling. Another person says they cannot even imagine going through such torture.

It is not whether you feel anxious about it. Most of us do. In fact, it is likely even as you are planning to break out of this social rut, that part of your brain is screaming at you with a bullhorn, "You'll never make it. You can't do this, it's safer to just stay home!"

The biggest single hurdle is a mental one. It is what happens in your head when you face any challenge. A confident person recognizes that the anxiousness they are feeling is normal, hesitates for a moment, and pushes through.

Yet my lack of confidence has convinced me that I would be humiliated, look foolish or get rejected. My fear of roller coasters centered around being out of control, which is exactly what some people love about it! At that moment, the fear of a loss of control is greater than the possible pleasure from stepping out.

Imagined Fears

Most human beings have natural fears of falling and loud noises as babies. We gather many additional fears as we grow up. Natural fears are here to keep us safe, yet many of the fears we learn over a lifetime keep us from growing to our fullest God-given potential.

I have a fear of heights. If I watch a guy on television mountain climbing or walking a tightrope, my heart races, and my palms get sweaty, even though I am sitting safely on the couch. Anxiety, shyness, and lack of confidence can easily elicit the same reaction. They all harbor fears. What are your fears keeping you from experiencing?

Anxiety could be called "imagined fear." Anxiety provides a set of movies that get played over and again in your head. Daydreams, past experiences, and concerns about the future all play into anxiety. These movies have the same effect as the golfer who visualizes a great swing to improve his confidence, but with the opposite result. You visualize again and again how this imagined fear will negatively impact our life. This fear then keeps you from trying.

The fear of ending up in another unhappy relationship had kept me from moving forward. Every time I considered the thought of dating again, images of worst-case scenarios would start playing in my head. With those thoughts, it didn't feel worth the risk.

While these imagined fears rarely have any real risk to them, you often respond with the same "fight or flight" reaction as if there was a real danger. That imagined fear plays repeatedly in your head, stifling your ability to act.

Our minds have a wonderful way of responding to real life danger without having to think through the process first, or most of us wouldn't have lived to this age. I remember walking through the woods one time and stepping on a snake. I stepped right in the middle of him, because both halves of the snake reacted, and I caught the movement out of the corner of my eye. Do you think I stopped to assess what kind of snake it was? Not a chance! As quickly as my eye caught the movement under my feet, I ran! After I had time to process what had just happened, I went back to see what kind of snake it was. It was a harmless garter snake. My body quickly reacted and moved me from a potentially harmful situation without any conscious decision-making on my part.

Whether it is true fear or imagined fear, your body cannot tell the difference. When you are in a life-threatening scenario, your brain releases adrenaline which is used up by the body in the process of saving your life.

Your body's response to anxiety is the same, but the energy released has no place to go since there isn't any real danger to run from. The stress builds up as you sit quietly, sweating bullets. You don't like the feeling, but don't know how to disperse it. Next time around, you put up walls so that you will not have to experience the discomfort again. These walls are erected to protect you but can easily become your own prison. These reactions take place in your life when you sense and respond on a subconscious level. It can save you in genuine life-threatening situations and hurt you when that fear is imagined such as anxiety. It begins to control aspects of our lives on a subconscious level.

What if you took the same energy used to construct walls to keep you safe and instead, used that energy to catapult you toward a more fulfilling life? It really takes more energy to keep up the walls than it does to tear them down. Taking down the walls that keep you from leading a more social life will reap rewards that far exceed your expectations. Action toward a solution over time will diminish anxiety and allow you to live a more purposeful and fulfilling life.

It is important to remind yourself that everyone worries. We all have fears. Most of us are afraid that we do not measure up. Military men and women, rock stars, great leaders, and heroes all experience these same fears at times. The key is to move forward anyway. In the following sections, we will discuss how to move from where you are to where you want to be.

Building the Foundation

We will build up your foundation of confidence one brick at a time. Visualize in your mind that each step you conquer, no matter how small you perceive it to be, is another brick in the foundation of your self-confidence. Each step you take through reading this book and doing the exercises in the companion course will push you to grow. Many will take you outside of your comfort zone. You will want to quit at times, but each step is a victory, another brick in your foundation of confidence.

It is important that you find success in each little accomplishment that is taking you closer to confidence, and social growth. Little accomplishments add up to big life changes. It is easy to only consider it a success after you have reached completion. The happiest people are those who can find joy in the little things in life and let everyday accomplishments be a victory. Don't overlook the accomplishment in those little achievements. Celebrate them! Whether you pat yourself on the back, or treat yourself to something special, allow yourself to enjoy these little triumphs every step of the journey. You will need to take part in each step to create any real change. The power to gain confidence is right inside your own head.

Deciding to Take Control

One major factor toward success is just showing up and doing what you already know you needed to do. Negative thoughts about who you are and the dating world around you can keep you stuck, afraid to reach out, and try the things you know you need to do.

CHAPTER 8
THE POWER OF YOUR PERSPECTIVE

"I wouldn't have seen it if I hadn't believed it."- Marshall McLuhan

I met Michael Fontana back in the late 1990s. Though he was several years younger than me, we shared a common love of photography. He would stop by to see me at the camera shop that I ran. When he came in the door, he always wore his signature smile. We would talk about our latest photographic adventures, and he would fill me in on people he was helping in the community. His mind and focus were on everyone else, and I never once heard him complain.

I remember overhearing someone else complaining about the terrible weather that we were having, and how he just could not stand the dreariness. Michael whispered to me "I have got too much to do to spend a moment worrying about the weather." I bet that most of us know someone like this, who you rarely hear a negative word from, whose spirit always seems to be high, and who can find the good in even the bad times.

This was just who Michael was. Michael wasn't a warm, optimistic personality because everything was going his way though. He had Duchenne's Muscular Dystrophy and had lost the use of his body from the neck down. He drove a motorized wheelchair, driven by a small stick that he controlled with his mouth.

It was an intense process just to get Michael out of bed and ready for his day. He always required someone's help. He knew his clock was ticking, because he had told me he already lived many years beyond what the doctors told his parents that he would. Michael had every reason in the world to be angry about his lot in life. He had every reason to be bitter, to feel victimized, and to say, "What's the use?"

Instead, he taught me how to maximize the time I had on earth, to reach for things I might not have, and to stop saying, "I can't." I never once heard him say anything negative about his life or anyone in it. His focus was on everyone else, on lifting other people up, and praying for them when they were down. That is the power of perspective. People like Michael are a special breed, and others are drawn to them. People basked in the sunshine that he created. This is something we can all learn from.

What is Your Perspective on Dating?

How you view dating and love is paramount to how you will approach getting back out there. Your perspective on stepping out controls your mood, your behavior, your body language and your decision-making. Keep this in mind as you consider your own perspective throughout these chapters.

Your Pair of Shades

Imagine yourself wearing a pair of gold-tinted glasses. When you peer through them, you see the world in a different color, far more vibrant than someone whose glasses are tinted a dreary gray. All of us have our own unique perspectives, each colored by our world, personality, and experiences. These perspectives tint our view of the world.

Your lack of confidence tints your world differently than that of a person with confidence. Past dating experiences, shyness, social anxiety, or lacking a social network also affect your perspective. Each of the experiences you have in life are viewed from your unique perspective, just as wearing colored glasses tint your view.

How you perceive any situation influences what you see in it, how you believe the situation will unfold, and how you feel about it. When an emotionally impactful event occurs in your life, it shapes your view, and that event changes how you interpret similar future events. In a real sense, that event changes the color of the glasses through which you view the world.

None of us truly see from a completely objective point of view. My past and my own biases will always play a role in my perspective, but I can learn to recognize how my unique perspective causes me to see things the way I do, and how that can positively or negatively affect my decisions and interactions with others.

Each of us has opinions of how the world works. These assumptions play a large part in coloring your world. If the two of us were in a room together, witnessing the same event, we each would see a different viewpoint and perspective. You have likely experienced this at some point yourself, you and a friend experiencing an event, but leaving with a very different story of what happened.

To each person, perception becomes reality. Even though it is a different reality than others in the room experienced. Your thinking, personality, and past life experiences color or cloud your perception of any event. Thus, each person lives out his or her own version of that experience. Your life, and every single event in it, is affected by your perception of it.

You have your own assumptions of the outside world, and other beliefs that are directed at yourself. These perceptions can make your world a wonderful place to live in, or leave you depressed, fearful, desperate, and anxious. Your brain scans the world around you, looking for the things you choose to focus on. It is up to you to decide whether to look for the negative, or the positive. There really are so many wonderful things about being alive today. Choose to look for the positive.

Thinking Self-Confidently

Having confidence allows me to better tackle life challenges and to go beyond the limits that would otherwise have stopped me and make the most of my God-given gifts. Confidence helps me to find and explore talents that I would have overlooked otherwise. Many of my limitations are in my mindset. My perspective is my reality. But my perspective can change. Deciding to change my perception of the world opens the door to see the things in a whole new light.

Developing a positive outlook on your entire life will enhance both your life, and the lives of those you touch. Having an optimistic life view will allow you to see the good in everyday life and help grow confidence. It will open your eyes to opportunities and advantages in the day-to-day. It allows you to be proactive to life instead of reactive to what is happening to you.

It's easy to say, but not at all easy to do if you are pessimistic by nature. Recognizing that your thought process naturally skews this way is the first step.

Your belief system evolves over the course of your life, and your everyday life operates around these beliefs. All this happens without awareness of it.

Your beliefs about yourself and the world around you control your perceptions and decisions. These decisions focus you in a certain direction. These collective decisions, stacked one upon the other, design your life, without you even being aware of it. This holds true not only in your dating life, but your entire life.

You may have things in your background that affect your ability to trust others. You may not be happy with your weight. You may be uncomfortable in social situations. You may be afraid of falling into another bad relationship. There may be many things that have kept you from moving forward. Deciding that today you will take control of the rest of your life is the very first step. Determine to take charge of what you can control. Instead of waiting for your future to happen to you, you can take steps that will put you in the driver's seat.

Here are a few questions to ask yourself if you struggle with this:

- Does my perspective of the world around me raise or lower my quality of life?
- Does my perspective of me keep me happy or unhappy?
- If my perspective changed, could I have a more positive impact on the world around me?
- Does my current perspective of me give me a chance to succeed?

How do I Begin?

Start by first attempting to look for the good in things. I'm not perfect at applying this technique myself, but here are some questions I've asked myself for years to look for the good in any situation.

- "What could I do to make the best of this?"
- "What can I do to give this a positive outcome?"
- "What's great about this situation?"
- "What could be great about this?"
- "What can I learn from this?"
- "How can I grow from this?"

These are a lot of questions to keep in mind when it comes to preparing your mindset. Commit to memory at least one of these, and you will be on your way. Start by memorizing and repeating, "What can I do to give this a positive outcome?" when you are in less than the ideal scenario. It gives you a purpose and control, and it comes from a positive position.

All these questions relate to the bigger question of "How do I make the most of this situation?" When you do this, you automatically reframe your thinking, and change the way you approach the situation at hand.

Another simple, but astounding change that you can do is to approach others with a smile. This puts you in a positive state and increases the likelihood of others coming from a positive state as well. Take note that I did not just say smile if someone first approaches you with a smile. Approaching others with a positive expectation and demeanor is life changing. This will feel false and awkward if this does not come naturally to you at first. That makes it no less life changing, however.

All this sounds easy, but it can be difficult depending upon the situation and your own personality. You will get better at this with practice. These are life-long journeys, and we evolve and grow throughout them. Work on these things and do not expect perfection. Don't give up on them when you don't get it right.

When you allow a transformation of your thought process to occur, the speed with which changes take place can be astonishing. When I change my perspective of who I am, my view of the entire world around me changes with it.

Whenever you catch yourself struggling with your thoughts on how hard getting back out there is, reframe your thoughts. If you are coming back from a breakup, reframing your though might sound like, "It is so great that I have the opportunity to start over, and really search for the very best partner for me. I won't shortcut myself this time." Reframing your concern can change the entire thought process.

You Find What You are Looking For

When I first set out into the dating scene, it was especially awkward. I remember discussing with friends that I was having meeting the right people, or any single people at all. Their response was usually about as pleasant as if they were describing having a root canal. "Good luck meeting anyone in this town" was a resounding, positive theme. The fact that many of my early dates felt awkward seemed to justify their statements.

Yet I knew I could not allow myself to believe what other cynics were telling me was true. I knew there had to be great single people out there. I just needed to figure out how to find them. In addition, I knew that if I believed that there were no good people out there, I would constantly find truth in that statement. We typically go through life justifying our own beliefs, consciously or not.

We expect to be right in our conclusions, so we subconsciously look for the things that "prove" we are.

"I'm too__________."

"All men want is_________. "

"People are_________."

"All women are___________."

Then we look for all the proof. If I believe the world is full of worthless singles, that is what I will find. If I focus on finding great people, I will find them. This is not a "law of attractions" statement. It is simply perspective. We like to be right, and believe our perspective is accurate, so we seek to confirm your own beliefs, good or bad.

Embarking Upon a New Path

There are a lot of new patterns that you are building here. As you do, you will constantly find yourself going back to your old, ingrained pattern. Have you ever moved your office trash can to a new spot? How many times did you catch yourself going for the old spot?

The same thing occurs in your mind when you develop a new thought pattern, a new approach to meeting people, or expanding your world in some other way. You must work hard at establishing a new mental pattern, and fight against the urge no matter how many times you catch yourself back in the old pattern. Once the new pattern has taken hold, it becomes ingrained, and your new pattern begins to feel just as comfortable. Don't give up while this new pattern is being established.

CHAPTER 9
CHANGE YOUR MIND AND TRANSFORM YOUR LIFE

"When you change the way you look at things, the things you look at change."- Unknown

Do you know that the single biggest difference in confident people isn't their IQ, how much money they make, or their looks? The common thread lies in their thought patterns. In this section, we will discuss both the ongoing dialogue that you have with yourself, and the movies playing in your head during any given day. When you are hesitant to reach outside of your comfort zone in dating "What if" seems to be the biggest concern. You ask questions like this:

"What if it doesn't work?"

"What if I get rejected?"

"What if my heart gets broken?"

Instead, I'll ask you this question," What if you try it, and it changes your life?"

How Do You Talk to Yourself?

Do you ever find yourself playing and replaying "movies" in your head throughout the day? Often these "movies" are of negative past experiences, or possible future situations that you have a concern about. It takes the form of a running commentary throughout your day. This inner dialogue lies just below the surface and just out of your direct consciousness. It is going on behind the scenes. You rarely argue against its claims. Regardless of whether your thoughts are of past experiences or future concerns, they take you out of being your best now.

The negative perspective I had toward each step to get back into having a social life was directly responsible for the level of dread I felt. The idea of dancing in public, for instance, was something I could not even consider the possibility of doing. The dread I felt was incredible. This all came from the fact that I had pondered how terrible it would be so many times, that my inner chatter was directly affecting my decision-making.

In psychology, this inner conversation is called self-talk or your inner dialogue. While it occurs subconsciously, it has a direct effect on our mood, thoughts, behaviors, and decisions.

Negativity

Are you able to live in the moment and enjoy life? Do you find you are always beating yourself up over past mistakes? Are you always worried about what bad thing is coming next? Most of us from time to time ruminate on past mistakes, future concerns, or a time in our life that we were "better" than we are now.

I was there. My own negative concerns regarding myself had crept back in after my divorce. I couldn't think past the negativity, but there were good things about me. I was just weighing the negative as so much more important than all the positives. The fact that I weighed the negatives more heavily didn't make them true, however.

If you have trouble motivating yourself to try something new, you probably have an internal monologue about that subject that is negative. When your self-talk is negative, you will find the negative in everyday life and in yourself. These thoughts can cause you to hesitate or quit before you even get started. Then you are not only less likely to accomplish it, but likely to never get off the couch to try.

The Company You Keep

If you hang around with negative people, it is likely that you will hear the same thing from them. People who are not happy often want to steal your joy and confidence from you. Realize when this is happening to you and separate yourself from them when possible. When you cannot do that, recognize that no one can make you unhappy unless you allow them to.

Consider the old saying that you are the average of the five people that you spend the most time with. A study, "The Spread of Obesity in a Large Social Network over 32 Years " published in the New England Journal of Medicine by Nicholas Christakis and James H. Fowler, showed that a person's chance of becoming obese increased by 57 percent if they had a friend who had also become obese. There was even an increased risk of obesity even if that friend's friend was obese. Our perception of what is acceptable changes with the company that we keep, and then our behavior soon follows suit.

Consider the company you keep. How do they affect your behaviors, decision-making, and what you consider acceptable? If they are working on their health, their financial situation, their spirituality, or any other area of their life, you likely will be doing so as well. If they spend their time in activities that are not helping them grow, you will naturally be pulled in a similar direction. You will grow in the direction of the people you choose to spend your time with. Choose them wisely.

Anxiety and the Company You Keep

If you deal with anxiety regularly, it is easy to find yourself in the company and comfort of others who also are dealing with anxiety. This can occur through other family members, or friendships you have made. You have found a sense of comfort in another person who does not push you outside of your comfort zone.

If you struggle with being uncomfortable in social situations, and you have a friend or family member that recognizes this, and aids in your avoidance of those situations, they are helping to keep you from growing beyond that. The longer you avoid anything that makes you uncomfortable, the harder it is to dig out of it. While it feels good to have someone close who understands, it will ultimately make your anxiety worse as you allow yourself to spend more time in that comfort zone, and less and less time in the real world.

If this experience sounds familiar to you, connect with people outside your comfort zone to help you push past what feels safe, and to grow in a healthy direction.

Changing Your Mind

We have all made plenty of mistakes. I have spent time with people who have made huge life mistakes in their lives but could forgive themselves and move on toward a better life. I have also met people who relive their mistakes daily and keep themselves from being able grow.

Which of these two viewpoints will let you grow and enjoy life? Which one will keep you stuck? Your past is permanent. Beating yourself up will not change a thing. You can decide to change the way you interpret and respond to your past. This gives you the chance to move forward.

I was the first member of my immediate family to be divorced. I wasn't proud of it. But now it was time for me to move forward. I wanted to make sure that my second marriage was to the right person and to grow from my past mistakes. Are you ready to move toward growth, or stagnate where you are because you can't forgive yourself?

I found it helpful to ask myself these questions:

- Is this thought true?
- How would my life change without this thought?
- Am I being too hard on myself?
- Am I jumping to conclusions?
- Am I expecting perfection?
- Am I overly tired, or overwhelmed in some other area of my life which is affecting my outlook?

Be aware of the way you talk to yourself.
Do you hear yourself making the following statements?

- I can't believe I did that again.
- I feel so stupid.
- With a body like that, no wonder I don't get asked out.
- I will embarrass myself when I get up in front of everyone.
- I'm such a bum!
- What a loser.

A negative view of myself is just as powerful as a positive one. It shapes my life every bit as much. Yet I can change this viewpoint. I have the choice of which viewpoint to focus on.

The everyday decisions I make are based on my beliefs of who I am. These choices determine the life I live, one decision at a time. Most life decisions are just little decisions, stacked one on top of the other over time. Remember that your thoughts and beliefs are not facts. They are your perceptions.

Once you can recognize your personal self-talk as thoughts instead of reality, you can:

- take away its power of influence.
- replace them with thoughts that encourage you instead.

The powerful thing I realized is that when I *think* I can do something; I look for things to prove my belief. When I *think* I cannot do something; I look for proof that it is impossible. When I allow the conversation in my head to become more positive, I give myself the opportunity to stretch myself, grow, and succeed. The key to getting started is realizing this and consciously reminding myself to focus on seeking out solutions and searching for the good in things.

Catch Yourself

Dating is an emotional roller coaster ride for nearly everyone. I would come home after a night out, feeling dejected if things hadn't gone as planned. In dating though, things rarely go as planned. To keep from giving up altogether, I found it helped to note the things I had done right, so I had something to celebrate along the way.

Your dating adventures will leave you feeling beaten up at times. You won't do everything right, trust me. But with each step, there are things you will do right. You need to keep an eye open for those, pat yourself on the back for the accomplishments made, and build on that for the next dating opportunity.

If you tend to be hard on yourself, it is time to begin consciously reframing your thoughts to find a solution instead of a putdown. The time to change your thinking is right now.

Thought Stopping

I first ran into Thought Stopping years ago when I was struggling with depression myself. When I would find I was thinking negatively about myself, or the situation, I would silently yell "STOP" in my head, and then reframe my thoughts in a positive perspective. Thought Stopping was first introduced to the world by psychologist Dr Joseph Wolpe. It is used in behavioral therapy to treat obsessive and phobic thoughts and can easily be employed when you find yourself struggling with repeated negative thoughts. I found this to be the simplest way to cut off a negative thought pattern and redirect my energy toward problem-solving.

Remind yourself that no matter how compelling the voice, or how many times you have heard it, that does not make it accurate. This technique is simple but effective. The more often you do this, the more effective you will find that this process becomes. When you recognize your self-talk and thoughts as simply perceptions, you can begin to allow your self-confidence to grow.

The Rebuttal

How can you rebut the voice in your head? Can a Bible verse help you? Can remembering a compliment that someone gave you help you? Can you tell yourself a positive statement about yourself?

Changing Your Inner Voice

There are five important steps to take in changing your inner voice:

Step 1: Be aware of the conversations you have, so you can stop yourself.

What do you beat yourself up for consistently, that affects your dating confidence?

One thing that affected my confidence was that in the digital age, portrait studios weren't as lucrative as they once were. I struggled with the feeling that I wouldn't be a good dating candidate because of the economic downturn.

Step 2: Consider the voice in your head as your inner Grinch. As you begin to catch yourself in internal conversation, change the voice. You can do that. It is the voice in your own head. That voice may sound like your own, or that of someone who put you down in the past. Change it. Make it sound comical. Imagine it as the Grinch's voice. Even if this sounds absurd, it helps break the nature of the voice that you have grown used to hearing. It helps you take this criticism less seriously.

Step 3: Stop yourself. When you hear that voice being negative about an aspect or situation, stop yourself with a silent scream that works for you. "Stop!" or "Quit it!" or "Knock it off" all work.

Step 4: Having consciously prepared beforehand, replace the negative statement with a positive, solution-based conversation. Since we typically follow the same habitual pattern of self-talk, having a prepared positive turnaround is often easy. What can you use as a rebuttal when you catch yourself?

Step 5: Begin looking for the things you do right, instead of focusing on what you feel that you lack. Each time you catch yourself, ask yourself if you are focusing on the problem or the solution. What can you say that is positive or encouraging to yourself? Each time the thought of not being a good dating candidate crossed my mind, I would remind myself that I am a loyal person, and that I find great joy in making the ones I love feel cared for. I also know that I am a tireless worker who loves to provide for his family. Reminding myself of these positive qualities helped snap me out of my negative focus.

Determine to do this each time you catch yourself. When you begin reframing the questions you ask yourself, you are on the way to change.

Reinterpreting Failure

When you focus on the problem or replay your past mistakes, you expend time and energy that could be used to create solutions. You cannot experience success without also experiencing failures. Failure is a great learning tool. Think back to times you've failed at something, and you will usually find you grew from it.

When you struggle with your confidence, you are much more likely to consider yourself a failure when things go wrong. The confident person, however, sees that same failure as an experience to be learned from. They don't like falling short either, but it is not seen as a personal failure. That is a distinct difference.

Instead of being critical of your mistake, you need to see it as a learning experience. It is a shift of perspective.

Do not take it as a personal failure. It's important to not beat yourself up repeatedly about falling short, and to keep moving forward. You need to allow yourself to make mistakes, but you are not your mistakes. Give yourself credit, even when plans do not work out the way you hoped.

When I make a mistake, I need to analyze it:

- Did I step out of my comfort zone and try something new? Rarely does anything go exceedingly well the first time we try it. I will give myself a break, and the opportunity to try again.
- Use the experience to grow. What positive thing can I take from this? What will I do differently next time?
- Do not make it personal. I am not a failure because of this.
- I need to give myself credit for stepping out and pushing myself, even if it did not turn out exactly as I had hoped.
- Owning my mistakes instead of turning the blame elsewhere is the

mark of a confident person. It's okay to fall short. If I am pushing myself to grow, I will make mistakes. Don't diffuse the blame. Accept it, own it, and keep pushing.

What Does all this Have to do with Dating?

When you try something new, you are going to make mistakes. That is natural. That's exactly what is going to happen in this new realm of dating. When things do not go as planned, the first thing you say is, "I knew this would never work." Making the decision to reframe these thoughts toward a positive perspective will keep you moving forward.

We all have strengths and weaknesses. Choosing to focus on your positive qualities keeps your mindset in a positive place and lessens the number of times that you will beat yourself up.

As we wrap up, let me ask you this question: "Which is a more powerful tool to propel you forward on this journey — a positive or negative mindset?" You know the answer. It is a positive mindset! It is the mindset that will allow you to express your true capabilities and not hold you back.

Make sure your self-talk is gracious and kind, as you would talk to a friend. Determine not to talk to yourself any differently than you would want anyone else to. I also like to remember what God has said about me. I am treasured, I am significant, I am capable, and I am valuable.

CHAPTER 10
FINDING HELP

"We struggle all our lives to learn the most basic things about ourselves even a casual passerby could tell us in a moment."- Anonymous

Who do you know that can help you feel more confident? Do you have a friend or coworker who is more stylish who can help to make sure your look is not out of date? Having honest feedback about how the rest of the world sees you can be eye-opening. This insight can be exceedingly helpful if you find it hard to date, meet people, or make friends.

Bring that friend onboard and let them coach you. Don't wait on this. Lady friends often would love to give someone a hand and enjoy being be a part of the matchmaking process. Sometimes there is just one thing that you cannot see yourself, that can make all the difference. Guys, this is just as important for you. Don't skip this step!

Can they help you with anything that you may not be aware of?

- Do you use profanity like it was your native language,
- bite your nails, or have other habits that need to be brought to your attention?
- Are you whiny or depressing to be around?
- Are you needy?
- Are you critical of everything and everyone around you?
- For Men, do women feel uncomfortable around you? The funny thing is the guy who makes women feel uncomfortable is often the

guy who would bet $100 that he doesn't.

- For women, does your friend notice that you come on too strong? Do you push good men away out of fear or anxiety?
- Is it time to update your hairstyle? Ask your stylist or find a new one. Guys, a lady with taste can help you massively! Take advantage of a friend's help and advice.
- Are you age wearing appropriate clothing? Are there things about your style that need updating?
- Are you maintaining adequate hygiene? This ranges from things, such as dandruff flakes to greasy hair, stained teeth, bad breath to sweaty handshakes. There are many things to consider.

Knowing these things could direct you to make small changes that add up to a big difference. Your appearance is the first impression that people have of you when they meet you. Clothing, grooming, and a friendly smile reveal who you are before others get to know you. When you encounter a store employee, waitress, or any stranger in a public scenario, you make determinations about this person in an instant. Other people are doing the same from what they can see about you.

While you cannot always judge a book by its cover, it is often all we have at first glance. People draw expectations and conclusions about you before you ever open your mouth. Take a personal inventory. What messages are you conveying to the rest of the world?

This exercise and thought process is to help you feel confident and prepared. It is not about becoming consumed with what others think of you. It is about realizing your clothing, actions, appearance, facial expressions, and words you use may tell a different story than who you really are. Let's get the two aligned.

Accountability

The friend that is helping you with appearance may help with accountability as well, or you can seek out someone else for this role. You should choose someone who can be both truthful and encouraging. They should be realistic, but able to look for and find the positive as they propel you forward. It is important to choose someone who is in a successful relationship. They should also share your personal beliefs. Agree to stay in contact regularly with your friend or coach to monitor progress.

Here are some sample questions to discuss together:

- What success have you had in meeting new people this week?

- In what ways did you step out of your comfort zone to achieve this?
- What did you learn from this success?
- Did you encounter a dating-related setback this week?
- What did you learn from that setback?
- What social goals have you set for yourself this coming week?
- What method will you employ to meet new people this week?

You can keep a notebook noting both achievements and setbacks, along with future dating goals. It will help you better recall your week and make it more likely to follow through with the calls, as you have been preparing for it all week. This does not have to take long. This is easily achievable in a five to ten-minute phone call each week.

Make your coach aware of just who it is you are looking for. Share with them the list you created of your Must-Haves and Deal-Breakers in Chapter 4: Who Am I Looking For? This way, you have someone checking in that is not emotionally attached to the people you are meeting. They can help to be sure that the people you meet really are the kind you want to spend your time with. This is especially important if you have not made good choices in the past or fall head over heels too easily.

Having someone to hold you accountable in these efforts, while allowing you to share both your positive and negative moments will be a true help. You are more likely to be successful in any endeavor when you are surrounded by supportive people. Having that support system will prove invaluable in your pursuit of a happier, healthier life.

CHAPTER 11
PLAYING IT SAFE

"May your choices reflect your hopes, not your fears." -Nelson Mandela

Although I am not a safety expert, I wanted to include tools and strategies that would give you a you a good overview of safety for both men and women. The more you know about safety the better.

We all have concerns about our personal safety. I don't want those concerns to keep you from getting back out there, though. With a little awareness and forethought, you can navigate the waters safely. While I don't intend to scare you, it's always better to be safe than sorry.

I have broken this into two sections, Online Dating Safety and Dating Safety. While these overlap in many areas, dividing them up creates awareness as you move from meeting online to meeting face-to-face.

Online Dating Safety

I'm sure you won't be shocked when I say this, but not everyone who is online is honest. The truth is though, you can meet those same dishonest people in-person.

You may meet:

- Liars
- Married people pretending to be single.
- People looking to con you out of money.

- Those who want to lure you into unsafe situations.
- People who are not who they represent themselves to be.
- And finally, many wonderful, honest people who are using this tool for good.

Our goal is to meet as many of the latter as possible, to the exclusion of the others. Following the tips in Dating Safety, along with the steps outlined will give you the game plan to help carry this out.

Before You do Anything Else:

- Create a new Gmail email without your name in it, just for online dating.
- With that new email, go to Google Voice www.voice.google.com, and create a Google phone number. This will allow you anonymity when you give out your phone number.
- Google yourself. You may be surprised by what you find, including others with the same name It's good practice for the time when you start Googling your potential dates as well!

When Using Online Dating Sites or Apps:

- When you create a username, don't use your name as part of it.
- Don't give out personal information online, such as where you live, where you work, or where you go to church. No need to share too much with people you've never met.
- Don't share your children's ages, what softball team they play on, school they attend, etc. Save the details for after you've met and feel comfortable with who this other person is.
- Don't post photos of your children. You could be sharing what your children look like with a pedophile.
- Check your privacy settings. Turn off location sharing on social media platforms. They can paint a clear picture of where you frequent by the frequency of photos shared from those locations.
- Use images not already circulating on business, organizational, or social media sites. Doing so allows others to find far more info than you would have want to share with a stranger.
- Get trained in using pepper spray. Then carry it!

When You've Met Online, but Haven't Met in Person:

- Again, consider the level of personal detail you are sharing, and do all your initial chatting on the site.

- Share your Google phone number when you two are ready to talk.
- Don't add them to your social media before you've gotten to know them. There is far more information about you on social media than most of us realize.
- Search your date online with whatever information you have gathered. Use Google, Facebook, LinkedIn, etc. Search the photos and see if they have been used by other people as well.
- Google their name and phone number. Another option is using the Been Verified App.
- Block and immediately report anyone that truly makes you uncomfortable or becomes abusive.

Scammers

If you meet someone online that asks for money or "help to go see a sick family member," stop corresponding with them and report them to the site immediately. This isn't a person you should feel guilty not helping. You've met a scammer. They come on charming, have amazing photos, are very conversational, and then pop the question into the conversation after they've warmed up to you.

It happened to me early on. Her pictures were very nice, and she was quick to strike up a conversation. Not only that, but there were no lulls in our conversation. She seemed very interested in me. Much more so than any other lady I had chatted with so far. It was exciting.

Then, out of the blue, she asked, "So you think you could help me go visit my mom who's sick in California?" I paused. I realized I was being scammed! When I told her "This is a scam!", It surprised me that she even apologized before disconnecting. Her profile had been taken down before I got finished reporting it. Reporting these scammers helps keep others who are using the site from becoming their prey.

Planning to Meet in Person:

- Always meet in a public place.
- Plan your initial meeting for coffee, tea or ice cream. This gives you an easy out. It is also a meeting where alcohol isn't typically part of the plan.

Dating Safety

The Initial Meeting

Tell a friend where you are meeting. Also, share the name, phone number and profile link of the person you are meeting. Set a time for them to check-in on you by text. Just telling your friend you are going out leaves them no information to go on if there was a problem.

Drive yourself to and from the date. Plan to meet in a public place: not your home, not theirs, and not in your neighborhood park. You don't know this person, even if you feel like you do.

Don't plan a hike, canoe trip, or anything that takes you away from other people. Play it safe and save it for after you've really gotten to know each other. Those with ill intent are often charming and convincing.

Stay sober, or don't drink at all. This isn't about being a prude. Once you really get to know this person, you can begin to let your guard down. If you choose to drink anyway, make sure that any drink arrives to your hand directly through the wait staff or bartender. Be sure to never leave your drink unattended to go to the restroom.

Cutting the Date Short

What happens if you meet someone, and you become uncomfortable? You can cut the date short by texting your friend a pre-planned keyword. This word will have your friend calling you with news that "you need to get home immediately". This lets you get out when you may have otherwise been hesitant to break off the date.

Other options involve getting up and having waitstaff escort you out, calling a ride, or having that same friend come meet you. How you get out is far less important than your safety. Don't feel bad if someone has set off your intuition. Always put your safety first, even when that requires being rude, or hurting feelings.

Get Home on Your Own

One last thought as your date ends. Don't let him drive or walk you home. Drive, or take an Uber. Remember, he doesn't know where you live. Don't show him; yet. Think about it like this; you go out with someone, and what you've shared with them is just your first name, a dating profile, and a Google phone number. If you don't like them, or get uncomfortable, you can block them on the site, and take no further calls from them on the

Google phone number.

But if you've shared your number, taken them by your house to meet your puppy, and added them as a Facebook friend, this person has far too much information you can't retract. The person may seem like your dream date in the chat and turn out to be entirely different in real life. You may wish you hadn't been so transparent once you've realized this. Play it safe until you get to know them. Remember, chances are none of this will matter — unless it does. Don't take the chance.

After you are back at home follow up on the info your date gives you. Does what this person tell you ring true when you visit their social media?

Is He Really Eligible?

As I mentioned before, it's a sad fact that not everyone you meet will be honest with you. In fact, there are those men out there that are married, and still playing the field, disguised as an eligible bachelor. Here are some tips to be on the lookout for as you meet men along the journey.

He Might be Married If:

- He can only meet at odd hours, or always at specific times.
- He will only meet in secluded places (which should raise all kinds of safety flags as well).
- He only wants to meet on a specific side of town or avoids your suggestion to meet in certain areas.
- He vanishes from contact with excuses about being "busy" with work.
- Things just don't seem to add up.
- All his transactions are cash based. He may not want to leave a paper trail.
- He doesn't want to display affection in public.
- You don't meet his family or friends.
- He pushes back when you want to move forward.
- There are special events you would expect to be invited to, but aren't.
- He has a tan line on his ring finger.
- He must be the one to initiate contact with you.
- He always prefers to meet at your place, and "stay in."
- You don't know where he lives, or you've never been invited there.

- At times he suddenly "has to leave" with no good reason. Does it happen more than once?

If the situations in which you can meet seem strange, it is not likely that he's an agent protecting world secrets for the CIA. It could be a sign that you are being played by a married guy. There is something up. Trust your gut on this one.

Tips for Guys; Making her Feel Comfortable on the First Date:

- Suggest meeting in a public place for her comfort.
- Make it a short activity, such as coffee or ice cream.
- Avoid asking questions like "Where's your house?" Or "What school do your kids go to?" or "What walking trail do you use?"
- Ask instead about her career, interests, musical taste, books, movies, and hobbies.
- Don't buy or offer drinks after she told you that she isn't interested.
- Don't pressure her to stay longer than she is comfortable.

CHAPTER 12
EXPANDING YOUR WORLD

"Twenty years from now, you will be more disappointed by the things you didn't do than by the ones you did do." - Mark Twain

People will say to you "You'll meet The One when you stop searching for them." It may work in the movies, but it's not a good plan. In fact, it is no plan at all. While it is possible to meet someone when you aren't searching, it doesn't increase the odds!

Most of the single people I met as I wrote this book seem to share many of the same viewpoints. Another common statement is that there is a tiny pool of candidates from which to find a date at all, much less a great partner. After all, the good ones are already taken, right?

This feeling comes partly because we have a limited circle of people which we know. If you are like me, you've pondered the single people you already know. And that list is way too small. But that's because of our limited viewpoint. It's not that there really are that few. In fact, there are an incredible number of single people, and many are hoping to meet someone like you. There are a few problems, however. One is that they also don't know you exist. And from their limited viewpoint, they don't see many eligible singles either. After all, they are saying to themselves "All the good ones are already taken."

There is a common statement in business that it is difficult to have a good viewpoint of your own business, or how to fix your business, when you are in the middle of your everyday work. From the middle of your everyday work it is hard to see the big picture. You are too fixed in the trenches. It is common to hear business speakers talk of looking at your business from 10,000 feet up. If you could see your business from a big picture vantage point and make big picture decisions instead of the decisions you make when you are just getting by, your business could change drastically.

How does all this apply to dating? If we could leave the ground in a helicopter and go just 1000 feet up, and your pilot could point out all the single people from that vantage point, you would be amazed. And if the same were repeated from 10,000 feet up, you would no longer feel the way you feel.

Now, I know this is a silly, impossible statement, but it does point out that there are far more single people of the opposite sex living near you than you can ever fathom. Yet there is still another problem. Many people aren't even looking. They've given up, or never gotten started at all.

Remember, your personal viewpoint is from ground level, and typically only considers those you encounter regularly. Yet this makes up a tiny fraction of the number of single people out there, many living just around the corner.

Matchmakers

In the old days, before the Internet and ready-made entertainment at our fingertips, we lived and socialized in communities. These communities were both a social and safety network. People looked out for one another and knew their neighbors by name. There were matchmakers. Matchmakers were people who knew the community's members and enjoyed connecting singles, hoping to make a love connection. It wasn't their career. It was more of a hobby.

Even in our busy world, there are many people who believe in love, and look for ways to connect singles together. They are great people to know. But if you don't know one, all hope isn't lost.

We all have people we work with, socialize with, or exchange goods and services with. And each of these people has a separate and distinct circle of folks they have contact with regularly. Even your closest friends have a distinct circle of contacts, though they may overlap with yours. Getting to know these people is a first step to expand beyond the circle of people you know.

My First Date Since High School

It was a blind date set up by my friend and fellow photographer Linda, that got the ball rolling for me. She had a client she felt was a good personality match for me. Linda did all the go-between and then connected us. I was both excited and scared at the prospect of getting back out there. What was interesting is that I'd never reached out to Linda to let her know to be on the lookout for me. She was looking out for me, nonetheless. She was playing the role of a matchmaker.

Once connected, we exchanged phone numbers, and began making plans. Christina and I met for the first time at a local restaurant. I have to say that my friend did a good job of pairing us up personality-wise. Christina and I enjoyed each other's company.

The positive start led us to plan a second date. We got along well. A few more evenings out to the movies and a football game. But those first few dates, along with some investigative questions had shown us we had different goals in life. I knew one day that I would want to get married again, and Christina was adamant that her name would never land on another marriage certificate in her lifetime. At that point we went our separate ways.

It would have been easy to make our personality connection work by overlooking our grand differences in what we were each looking for in life. Yet knowing my deeper needs helped me realize this fit wouldn't have worked for either of us.

What I had though, was a positive first date. I had found that I liked Christina's personality, and this initial success had gotten me off the couch and into the dating. My friend's setup of a blind date had set the stage for me to expand my world.

Get Started

Start by letting your friends, coworkers, family members, and others you associate with know that you are looking to get back into the dating world. Some will be more helpful than others. Some may have immediate suggestions, and others won't have anyone come to mind immediately. Don't give up just because of that.

It is important to discuss who you are looking for when talking with anyone that might introduce you to others. Once you've given them the details they need, tell them to let you know of anyone they think could be a good candidate for you.

This isn't a desperate act. This is growing your circle of prospects. You may be inclined to skip this because it feels uncomfortable, but each of the methods I'm prescribing throughout this book will bring you in touch with people you won't likely find anywhere else.

With your friends' knowledge of you both, there is an increased chance of common ground between the two of you. At the very least, the odds are better that you won't get connected to a terrible choice. Blind dates don't always make a love connection. Neither does any other method of meeting people, but they are a great head start to meeting people just outside of your own circle.

One of my lifelong friends met his wife in exactly this manner, and there is no way to count the number of people who have met their partner through this simple, direct method. Don't overlook the power of a blind date.

What I Learned from Blind Dates

- Who knows you better than your friends and coworkers?
- •Your friends know people outside of your circle. Each person you are introduced to opens a new circle to you.
- The more you open up to friends and people that you know, the more likely you will be introduced to new people.
- Many people run from the idea of a blind date, but if you set it up instead for a meeting for coffee, you get the power of a blind-date without having to spend an entire evening together

Getting the ball rolling is always the hardest part. Asking your circle of influence to assist you in getting things started is a good first step in the right direction. Once you've taken the initiative to ask those around you, this process doesn't require a lot of proactivity on your part. They will handle the follow through of getting you two connected. Blind dates are often the simplest method to take to get moving in the right direction.

As we move into the next chapter, remember your friends and coworkers, and their connection to people you have never met. If your family members and friends are pressing you to get back out there, tell them to find you some eligible prospects that fit your life-long partner criteria. This may seem like an old-fashioned way to meet people, but it comes with some very positive bonuses. Don't overlook this for all its possibilities.

CHAPTER 13
ADVENTURES IN ONLINE DATING

"Sometimes the smallest step in the right direction ends up being the biggest step of your life." - Denise Wood

When online dating first emerged, it was looked at negatively. People did not like to admit that they had met in such a way. That has all changed. Online dating is now so popular, people are often surprised if you didn't meet there. It is now embraced as a legitimate way to meet others.

Now that I'd taken my first step back out into the dating world, I decided I would increase my possibilities by looking into online dating. I set up a profile on a few free sites and tried out a free preview of Match.com. Some sites allow you a free experience, and others let you get a look at what's out there, but with little or no communication until you've paid up.

Looking back, I had no idea what I was doing. I paid up for a month of Match.com. "Why do the multi-month plan?" I thought. "It won't take long to meet some new prospects, and then I'll be set." I made a quick profile and posted to the site and sat back to wait for the messages to come in from interested prospects. I waited twenty minutes and checked. There was nothing. "Well, I need to give this to the end of the day," I thought. But a day later, I still had nothing. This trend remained steady for a week. Suddenly, I started to over-analyze myself. I wondered, "What is wrong with me? Not a single message from an available lady?"

At this point I had joined an online dating site, slapped up a few words on a profile, included no photos, and was surprised to get no response. That statement alone probably tells you I had a lot to learn.

I am a bit embarrassed to share this now. But I am sure I couldn't be the only single person out there who was beyond clueless on how all this works. After all, I was trying to recreate a social life that had gone away when Ronald Reagan was still president. My first attempt at cyber romance was scoring zero. It was then I realized I might need to figure out how all this worked.

I had a lot to learn. But over time, I realized online works. It gives you the ability to be in front of more people than any other single source. There is no other method that can match its power and reach.

Getting Started

Let me break down what I learned in my online experience, to guide you through getting started. The exact order of setup is determined by the dating site or app, and each one is different. The following guide will get you started, help keep you from making many of the mistakes I did, and give you tips to create a successful online experience. Keep in mind, technology is always changing.

This is less about what tool to use to take you where you want to go, and more about creating a connection to the outside world. The tools will change but understanding what makes you connect with others will not.

Creating Your Profile

As we begin, our main goal here is to let others know about our positive qualities that make us an interesting person. Remember the list that we started before. What we write, and how we word it, can be the difference between meeting others, and turning them away. In order for this to lead you toward the kind of person you want to meet, you will have to put in the time. Doing so substantially increases your odds of meeting the right people!

Though it took a while to get the hang of it, I eventually learned to create a profile that told an interesting story, gave a glimpse of who I was, and painted a picture of the person I wanted to meet. This helped me meet more of the type of people I was searching for and minimized the number of meetings that were doomed from the start.

I made sure mine sounded upbeat, as that reflects my personality. I mentioned my hobbies, so whoever read it knew some of the things I enjoyed. I discussed activities I engaged in, including being active and staying fit. I made sure to note that I was looking for someone to enjoy my life with (insinuating that I was not looking for a quick fling).

I also tackled another area of my life that I think was important to share in my profile. I don't drink alcohol. This isn't a religious statement as people often think, but instead it was from early life examples I saw as a young boy that turned me away from ever even trying it. I am aware that makes me an oddball in American culture. While I did not mind meeting someone who enjoys a drink now and then, I had no desire to engage in regular weekend drinking games with my future partner. It simply wouldn't work for me.

I made sure my profile stated that, but without a rant. I would mention in my profile that I truly enjoy life, but just don't drink alcohol. At times I got ridiculed online by those reading my profile. I had ladies say to me "You are obviously a recovering alcoholic; why else wouldn't you drink on the weekends?" I considered removing that from the profile, but in the end I met the perfect person for me.

Did that statement lower the number of people I met? I am certain it did. But it increased the likelihood of dates with the right people, because they knew up front. I didn't make statements like "No drinkers of alcohol need apply!" I marked in my preferences that I rarely or never drink in the searchable categories that most dating profiles offer. Did it stop me from meeting and dating others that enjoyed an occasional drink? Possibly, but I know it had an influence on who I met in a positive way. Looking back, I wouldn't change a thing.

Talk positively About:

- Who you are as a person (convey your personality.)
- What moves your heart.
- Your hopes for a future with someone you love.
- Who you are looking for.

I suggest you begin by jotting down a list or creating an outline of these four items, and how they pertain to you.

Use most of your writing to tell about who you are and what endeavors you enjoy: keeping fit, going to concerts, woodworking, going hiking, painting. Spend a smaller portion of your essay writing about things you hope to find in a mate. "I'd love to find someone who enjoys ________________."

What to Do:

- Your profile should be 75 percent about who you are, and about 25 percent who you are looking for.
- Are you witty? Are you serious? Does this show in your writing? I always preferred to inject a bit of humor into my profile writing when I found the chance, because that's who I am.
- If you can create a compelling short story of your profile, this can really make it stand out amongst the many others out there. As you write, inject your personality into the story.
- Being memorable isn't just a good thing; it's critical to keep your profile from getting lost among the vast number of profiles out there.
- People migrate toward optimistic people, and negativity repels nearly everyone!
- Include your hobbies, and things you enjoy doing.
- Are there places you enjoy visiting, or hope to visit one day?
- Do you have a funny story, or insights into who you are that allow the reader to connect with you? This will make you memorable in a sea of profiles.
- Check your grammar. Typos and misspellings will stand out as a definite negative.
- Use summarized, concise paragraphs. It will really help to show that you put in a real effort, and that this is serious for you.
- Do you have a few close friends who could read it, and offer suggestions? At least one of the opposite sex will offer insight you may have overlooked.

Mistakes to Avoid:

- Don't skip the profile. Guys, you decrease your odds of meeting good candidates drastically when you leave out the profile. Nothing says shallow more than a guy with just photos to show for himself.
- No unrealistic shopping lists here. If you state that you love a man in uniform, expect that you just excluded every man who doesn't wear one.
- Leave out rants about previous relationships and the kind of person you *don't* want to find on here. Be positive in your statements about you and what you are looking for.
- Don't appear too eager or needy in your writing. You want to be sure not to convey any sense of desperation or urgency in your

message.

- Leave out profanity.
- Don't forget to use a spellchecker!

It is easy to run good candidates away by being far too strong in your statements, be it political, religious, environmental or otherwise. I am not in any way telling you to hide your views, or back away at all from your principles. Your profile should not sound like a hardline rant, however.

You can push good people away by what seem like extreme views, when you are simply trying to state what you believe. It's not always easy to discern the difference between a belief and extremism in a dating profile. This isn't a concern for every online dating member, but it happens.

I read the profiles of several people whose criteria matched with mine, but their hardline statements told me things could be too rigid to enjoy life with. I am sure many, if not most of these people are great people, but the way they stated their viewpoints bordered on frightening. Again, have a couple trusted friends of the opposite sex read the profile you've written (always a good idea anyway) to be sure it conveys you in a positive light.

How Long Should My Profile Be?

There is no hard and fast rule on the length of your profile but try to wrap it up in 200-400 words. If it's too long, it feels like a novel. On the opposite end of the scale, just writing two to three sentences gives the reader the sense that you didn't put any real effort into it.

Say it With Feeling

When you read an article in a magazine, you quickly lose interest if it isn't attention grabbing. Your profile isn't just an opportunity to list your "specs", but a chance to make another person feel something when they read it: to be intrigued. By reading your profile, how will they feel about you?

For Men

Your profile is what women will use to determine whether they bother responding to your initial contact. As much as many of us would love it, most women still often leave the pursuit up to the guy.

Women often look for signs of courageousness and risk-taking in a potential mate. If you don't see yourself as the heroic type, you aren't out of luck. Weave some adventures into your storytelling and leave out that you prefer to sleep in footie pajamas until after she gets to know you better.

For Women

Men respond positively toward women who;

- show kindness
- care about staying in shape
- make themselves approachable
- have attractive pictures

Tell the Truth

Be honest in the statements you make about yourself. Do not lie about your age, your income, your marriage status, or anything else. This will always come back to haunt you. Lying on profiles (white lies included) is more prevalent than I ever imagined. One running enthusiast told me about the experience she had with meeting a marathon runner online. When they met in person, he was sixty pounds overweight, and it was obvious he hadn't been running in some time, if ever. He could have been a great guy, but the date was off before it ever got started because she felt she'd been lied to.

These kinds of inaccuracies occur all the time. If you don't like when they happen to you (and you won't), don't do it to others. Get started on the right foot with honest statements and observations about who you are and be sure your photos are current. It will go a long way toward finding a genuine match, and someone who will want to get to know more about you when you meet face-to-face.

Make Things Easier for Yourself

Create your profile using a Word, Notes, or Google doc, and copy and paste it to multiple sites instead of reinventing the wheel each time. I found that I had to make the formatting look nice once I copied it over, but it saved tremendous time over writing a new profile for each site. This method also allows you to run a spellcheck on your work before you put your masterfully written essay out there.

The Importance of Great Images

The current version of online dating is structured around the phone app. Here, photos of a prospect come up and you swipe right if you have an interest, or swipe left to discard them. While this allows you to move through prospects at an incredible rate of speed, it removes any depth, and makes this an entirely appearance-based tool. If that last statement has you discarding the idea of online dating altogether, don't toss it out yet. It really isn't that different from when you meet someone in person.

I realized that when I would go to any social gathering where I had the opportunity to meet people, most of those initial meetings involved appearance-based connections too. If I saw someone I had an interest in at any kind of gathering, most often it was based on appearance. Once I would meet them, I had the opportunity to dig a bit deeper. Realistically, there is only so much you can glean about a person prior to a conversation with them. Most of what we all have to go on in those first few minutes is whether or not the person is attractive to us. Not much different than the first step in a dating app.

If you take the time to dig into their profile section, the person on a dating site has given you some clues to their personality. This often gave me more detail than I would have gotten in a face-to-face meeting at a social gathering. There are advantages and disadvantages of any method of meeting other single people. Don't toss out online dating before you even get started.

While we know that starting a relationship based on looks isn't the ideal way to go, it really is no different than seeing someone at a park, or a party, and beginning a conversation. These are also superficial interactions, often based on appearance only.

Even with its inherent negatives, online dating increases your odds by sheer volume and connections you might never make in everyday life. There are many wonderful people using this tool to search for a companion. Don't miss out on meeting one that's right for you.

Your Photos

Where do we begin? Good, current photos of you are imperative. Members have nothing short of a sea of faces to scroll through to find you. The profile photo is often the only thing that gets seen. The choice of that first profile image is far more important than you may want to believe.

Enlist a Friend's Help

If you followed my earlier advice, you have a friend with good fashion sense helping you. The best place to start is your phone. Mark any photos of you alone as favorites. Gather images others may have taken of you as well. This is your starting point.

Your friend can be a big help here because the images you choose of yourself may not always be the best choice for your profile. We are often way too hung up on our own shortcomings. Having an objective opinion from someone you trust will open your eyes to images you might have dismissed. Your images are what makes the searcher decide to stop and go deeper.

Find someone with a good eye to help you create new images as well. It is fine to hire a professional photographer to help you capture images for you, but you should be seeking images with a casual feel without an overly polished look.

Take many images so you have plenty to narrow down from. Be sure to capture some full-length, waist up and head & shoulder length options, spending the most time and energy on the head & shoulder length.

A Story in Every Image

Show photos that help tell your story. Do you have images of yourself backpacking, traveling or on other adventures? What about photos that show your creative side, such as images of you creating art or engaging in a hobby? Do you have any photos of you playing sports or a musical instrument? Images that show who you are, and what you enjoy doing offer excellent stories and insight into your personality and interests. Images that show you being active are always a plus.

If you are a pet owner, including a photo of you with your pet is a clear statement for those who may be allergic or aren't fond of pets. Don't waste valuable real estate by including a picture of your pet alone though.

With the help of your friend, narrow them down to your top fifteen, of which you will select five for now. Be sure to include at least one head & shoulder view, along with one full-length image. Feel free to Include one image that shows you enjoying the company of other people if it won't cause confusion.

Videos are now an option as well. Make sure the video reveals something about your personality or an activity that is part of your life. Make use of this, as it's another area that sets you apart from the rest.

Own It

When it comes to choosing your profile photos, a consistent question from those concerned about their size is how much to show in their photos. Own it! The more comfortable you appear with yourself, the more attractive you appear.

- If every image is from an extreme up angle, the person on the other end will wonder why. Don't put neck-up shots online without also following up with full length and ½ length shots.
- Get it out there so there is no guessing.
- Show flattering pictures that show, or at the very least, hint at your size.
- Be positive in your attitude.
- Being upfront is far more empowering than surprising someone when you meet. You will feel more confident in meeting and far more likely to go through with plans to meet.

Putting a full-length photo on, even if you don't love the way you look, shows you are being upfront. It is truly empowering and limits the concerns about rejection that might come later because you weren't upfront to begin with.

If the person on the other end doesn't want to date you because of what they see, you don't really want to date them either! Do you really want to get the date by hiding something now, that ultimately will show when you meet face-to-face?

It is important for both guys and ladies to have images that are favorable, but realistic to who they are. And it is important to only use current photos even if you think you haven't changed.

A few Thoughts When Choosing Images

- Smile! People gravitate toward other happy people.
- Show images of you playing a sport or otherwise being adventurous.
- Offer one image that's more artistic, such as a black & white, or from a creative angle.
- Consider an image looking off, instead of at the camera, especially for women.

- Include a photo that feels fun, or hints at your personality.
- Show an image involved in a creative activity that you love, such as playing a musical instrument.
- While it never hurts to include a professional photo, most of your photos should have a candid feel. This will feel more real to the viewer.
- What about images that show you with others people? If they show you with members of the opposite sex, or if it's not easy to determine which person is you, leave it out.
- Include full-length, closeup, and head and shoulder length photos for variety.

For Men

I cannot tell you how many times I have been told by women they don't enjoy scrolling through images of you that include a dead animal. I know this seems like a great idea to a hunter, but for most ladies, it's not as appealing to as you may think. As a hunter or outdoorsman, you should show those activities. But may not need to include what you just shot. I can't speak for every female here, but I've been told that enough to make a note of it.

Leave out the shirtless selfies of you in the mirror. If you include a beach photo of yourself without a shirt on, that's fine. Just because you can include a shirtless photo doesn't mean you should. Again, your final selection of images is likely to improve if you have guidance from someone of the opposite sex.

For Women

Sexy poses with revealing clothing will garner attention on your profile from guys. These poses will have a negative impact on the quality of the prospects, however, reducing the number of serious seekers you hear from. Serious prospects are the only thing you are here for.

Do your photos portray you as a lady that he will want to introduce to his family, or one that would just be fun for an evening? If sexy poses are what you show, expect him to want to hook up. Don't expect it to turn into more.

Be sure to do the following:

- place your most striking photo as your main profile image.

- use a head & shoulder image, best suited for the smaller screen size viewing.
- choose a profile image in which you appear friendly and approachable.

As more apps come onboard using a swipe left or swipe right approach, it is more likely than ever that an initial assessment is made just from the first image. Make it a good one!

Be Sure to Avoid:

- Hiding your eyes behind sunglasses.
- Photos of you with a drink in your hand in every photo (unless that sums up your life).
- Posing with someone that could appear to be a significant other. Avoid using photos that include people of the opposite sex in general.
- Bathroom mirror selfies. They lack appeal. Leave them out.
- Background clutter. Is your house a complete mess behind you? I've seen many selfies where all I could focus on was the incredibly messy room in the background. These details leave an impression.
- A photo of your pet by himself. It's fine to include one with you and your pet. In fact, I think that's a good idea as a true pet lover. Just leave out the picture with Fido by himself.
- Photos of you with your children (an issue of safety).

Update Regularly

Regularly updating your photos can have positive effects. Some apps move you up the scale when you post a new image, so it gives both new and old visitors a chance to see your updates. Don't get missed because you never updated your photos.

If you've been on a dating site or app, you know it can be overwhelming at first. With so many potential candidates, it is common for members to go through their candidates again and again over the time they are members, scanning for new faces. I quickly got used to the faces I'd already seen, passing right by those that had become familiar. But a new photo would catch my eye, even if I would have passed them by previously. It can draw new attention, a profile read, and possibly a message sent your way.

A Final Note on Photos

Consider everything you put online as your dating real estate. Don't waste any of it. Like it or not, photos are the single most important factor in having others find you.

Don't let this part overwhelm you. Pick the best of what you have and get your profile online. Don't turn this into a two-week decision. We will be updating these photos anyway, so what you choose isn't a 'forever' decision. Move on this step today and give yourself 48 hours to make it happen.

CHAPTER 14
SELECTING YOUR SEARCH CRITERIA

"Sometimes the very thing you're looking for is the one thing you cannot see."
- Vanessa L. Williams

We live in a society that is all about speed of results. Online dating gives us a tool that allows us to not only meet people we would otherwise never meet in person; it gives us the ability to meet people at breakneck speed. This creates a very 'results oriented' energy around all we do within its borders. Understanding the benefits and pitfalls of meeting others at this speed can help steer you in a direction to make this tool work to your benefit.

Don't Cross Too Many Off Your List

When you sign up for many of the popular dating sites, you will have options to check for your preferences for who you are interested in meeting. Here you can state what religious background, interests, education and so much more. Always be sure that if you can knock out deal-breakers in this area (for example, a non-smoker), always do so.

But remember, the more criteria you place in your searches, the lower the number of potential matches you will have. Every single area you check a box in, set a height requirement on, or otherwise select, you are crossing people off your list...some potentially great people. Include criteria that are essentials for you but be sure not to narrow beyond essentials.

When I first got started, I was very stringent on my criteria selection. As just one example of being too picky, I marked that I would only be interested in dating people my age or younger 35-45, as I was 45 at the time. I didn't think anyone my age could keep up with me. What I found in time were many people a few years older than me that I ended up dating and enjoyed spending time with. Changing my profile to reflect that allowed me to meet more great people I would not have met otherwise.

The person you leave out by making too many criteria selections may be a wonderful candidate. Again, it's a numbers game. To find the pearl you are going to need to crack into a lot of oysters!

If you've been on the online dating game a bit, and feel your choices are too few, revisit the criteria you initially checked off when searching for potential suitors.

Be Age-Appropriate

Watch the age range you are setting in your interests. I consistently see men who search for women 20-25 years younger than themselves. There are several problems to consider before you do.

- You may struggle to find anything in common with these women, if you even find one who is interested in meeting you.
- You increase the number of women who are attempting nothing more than to scam you.
- You are likely to turn off women who are in your realistic dating range by hunting for girls the same age as their daughters. They write you off as a creeper and have no desire to interact.

Keep your age range within ten years of your own, and you'll meet people you have more in common with.

Little details can Derail a Match

Too much emphasis can get placed on the tiny bits of information you can learn because you don't have a lot of information to go on. You read through a profile, making snap decisions on others. Some of it is very helpful. But you can easily do this based on insights you judge more important than they really are.

The apps condition you to scan profiles at high speed, so you can make a "yes or no" decision in milliseconds. This pattern of thought sets you up to weigh insignificant details in your quest for the perfect partner. Music and movie preferences, for instance, aren't things that will play any significant part of your overall happiness with another human being. But in the quest for that perfect match, you may find yourself weighing less significant factors like they are deal-breakers.

You will do this to others, as you scan through profiles, and others who land on your profile will do that to you. You may love Will Ferrell movies. That is great, but someone who might otherwise be a wonderful match may skip right past you over this tiny tidbit, because she can't stand the guy. It's not likely that Will Ferrell flicks are on your lifelong "must haves" list. It may be better instead to state, "I love spending Friday nights at home with a good comedy." You can deal later with the trivial fact of your love for Will.

This illustration is a real-life example of how I almost never met my wife. In earlier versions of my own online dating profile, I noted that I love comedy movies, and had listed Will Ferrell type movies in there. Fortunately, that notation had gotten cut in later revisions of my profile. My wife tells me that if Will Ferrell had been listed in the profile, there is no way we would have ever responded to me. She would have written me off over that one small statement.

It sounds silly when you see it here, but statements like this, and "I couldn't bring myself to date a guy who wears socks with his sandals" happen all the time. Too many important positive traits can be overlooked in the "bad socks debacle."

Cynde and I are a great match but may have never met had that simple statement been left in my dating profile. As a side note, I still watch "Elf" every year at Christmas, though it's usually by myself.

At first it may seem that loving the same music might be important, but it rarely is. Unless your hobby is spending your summer camping out at bluegrass festivals, or you make your living as a roadie for a band, the exact genre of music may not be as important as the fact that "music inspires me." Yes, we want to have an honest profile, and information is good, but you don't want to turn someone away over what can seem important at the moment, but what ultimately wouldn't be a factor at all in your life with someone else.

I'm not asking you to hide who you are or what you like to do. Be sure to share all the important things in your profile. Just consider whether the things you are sharing are relevant to meeting the right person or could inadvertently turn them away.

Remember this when you are searching profiles as well. On a profile, there is no chemistry involved, unlike when meeting face-to-face. The very people you exclude over a trivial thing could be quite intriguing on a date.

Examples of Good Exclusion:

- You don't drink, and the online prospect has fifteen photos, fourteen of which include a beer in hand.
- You enjoy church, and have your children in church school, but she's an atheist.
- You enjoy a smoke-free lifestyle, so you should exclude smokers.
- You are allergic to pets, so you should avoid dating pet owners.

Examples of Bad Exclusion:

- He likes rock and roll music, but you prefer country.
- She loves college football, but you aren't interested.

My wife would surely have excluded me on the facts that I love to listen to loud rock and roll music; "Dumb & Dumber" is still among my top 10 all-time favorite cinematic gems; a normal TV volume is about 9 on a 10 scale; I love theme parks; or that I always love to be on the go.

But those exclusions would have meant that we would never have met. How different both our worlds would be today. Be sure that you don't "look" for things to remove others, but that you instead seek those with possibilities, and 'leave the excluding' until after you have met face-to-face.

Dating isn't something we are skilled at right from the start. Increasing the number of dates you have will hone your skills and make you better and less anxious in the process.

Who Takes the Lead?

Gentlemen, one thing I mentioned earlier is that us guys must be proactive online. Only occasionally did I have a lady reach out to me first on any dating site. As much as many of us guys would love it, there are many women who won't write to men without first being contacted.

Nearly all the correspondence I ever got online was after I'd made contact with her. This will vary by age group and is likely to evolve in time. I would have loved lots of interest from women just from having a profile out there, but it didn't work that way for me.

These are not at all my rules or suggestions. This is just the way it happened for me and the men that I talk to. The women I have interviewed for this book had the same consensus...most left the pursuit to the guys.

Gentlemen, since you will not likely get pursued online as much as you hope you will, you will take on the challenge of reading and responding to potential interests on your chosen dating sites. It is not uncommon for men to get responses from only ten to fifteen percent of the prospects they write to. It sounds disheartening, but I want to give you the tools to improve on these percentages, and the knowledge that it isn't just you.

Let's break this down fully, to give you some realistic numbers to expect. If you write to 100 ladies, you may only get replies from 10-15 of them. Why? Some profiles are "dead," meaning the person is now in a relationship but hasn't closed their profile. Some will not have an interest in you, and still others are just testing the waters, and rarely respond. Of that 10-15, chances are you will only get to meet 3-6 of those initial respondents for coffee. Writing to a lot of ladies is now your homework project.

When I first started sending messages, I was doing so one or two at a time, and I was waiting for a response before moving down the list. Wrong way to go about it unless you love to beat yourself up. It was a humbling experience until I realized that this is the norm.

Having these reference points and percentages to work from, do not allow it to discourage you. Instead, keep moving forward by:

- continuing to improve your profile essay
- continuing to update photographs
- not narrowing the field of candidates too severely through criteria selection
- making good first impressions through the wise use of messaging.

CHAPTER 15
THAT FIRST MESSAGE

"The most difficult thing is the decision to act, the rest is merely tenacity."
- Amelia Earhart

What's the first step to take once you've found someone you have an interest in writing to? Write to them! For some dating apps, to correspond both people must have shown a mutual interest. For others, it's a matter of writing and hoping the person on the other end responds. With eHarmony, the selections are made by eHarmony's profile matching system first, before any interaction can take place

When the time comes to send out a message to an interesting person, how can I know what to say? Though many of the same tips apply regardless, let's break it down between men and women.

What to Write Her

When you have found someone to write to, it is important to understand you may be one of many people that is writing that person. Setting your message apart from all the others that she is receiving, as one worth responding to, is crucial.

The first step is to show that you took the time to read her profile, and that you didn't message her after seeing her photos. Most ladies would like to know that you went beyond her physical appearance in choosing to write. Start by including a notation in regarding what caught your attention about her profile (other than her photographs). This comment tells her you took the time to read what she wrote, and that alone shows you are a more serious candidate, worth paying attention to.

Women get messages from guys commenting on their photos without having taken the time to read at all. Those with the best profile photos get plenty of messages from guys and must weed through them. Many are getting messages that are a copy and paste to a hundred other ladies. Too often, these messages are one line long, with nothing personalizing them. Nearly 100 percent of these types of messages end up in the recycle bin.

It will be different though when she gets a message from you. You have taken the time to view more than just the photos, and you mentioned something you found interesting within her profile. In addition, you have misspelled nothing, and you left an open-ended question for her to reply to. These simple steps have just increased your odds.

Will you get a reply from everyone because you followed these guidelines? No, but if you double your odds of a reply with every message, you will put yourself in another category altogether. You always want to stand out from the others, and this is one important way to do so. You need that initial message to catch her attention. Yes, it is a lot of work, but it can pay off handsomely.

Use these bullet points to get you started quickly. You will develop your own style once you've sent a few messages.

- Begin with "Hi" or "Hello". Or skip the salutation, and jump right in with "How's it going?"
- Tell her what caught your attention about her profile, or what moved you to write to her. Even if her physical attractiveness initially caught your attention, now is not the time to discuss it.
- Do you share an interest? If you do, start there. If not, mention the things she is passionate about that sound interesting, or that you'd like to know more about.
- Remember, starting this conversation shows confidence. And starting this conversation gets you off the sidelines and into the game.
- Ask an open-ended question that can give her something to reply to, such as:
- I'm curious what…
- Have you ever…
- I noticed that…
- Keep it short; 3-4 sentences is a great conversation starter. Save

your other thoughts for replies.

- Finish with something like "I look forward to finding out more about you. Write back when you have a chance."

(Your name)

What Not to Do

All of these are real examples and get used all the time by guys.

- Don't use internet slang or text abbreviations in your messaging. The reader is making judgements about you by the words you choose.
- Don't include your phone # and ask her to call.
- Don't send her photos of you.
- Don't ask her out.
- Don't tell her how pretty she is.
- Don't tell her you want to marry her.
- Don't tell her you want to whisk her away to a desert island.

This is a warmup message. Realize that when you find a great profile online with fantastic photos, you are one of many who have found her. Learn how to make your initial contact work positively for you. Make it stand out from all the others in a sea of messages and improve your odds. Don't just be another face in the crowd or creep her out by being too forward on the first exchange.

What to Write Him

You may have been told that men don't enjoy being pursued by women, and therefore you shouldn't message a guy unless he initiates it. I've heard the arguments too. While some men want to always be the pursuer, I feel this is more of a personality issue, and not a blanket statement. If you are only seeking a guy with a strong Alpha-male personality, leave the pursuit to him. But many guys enjoy the flattery and are happy to receive messages from a lady.

As you may have already found, some apps give women more control than ever, which is good. As I'd mentioned before, while I personally would have loved it if women had been messaging me on dating sites all day, every day, it wasn't the norm. This likely has much to do with age group, so younger people may not find the same issue.

You can use all the same tips noted above for men when writing, whether you are starting the conversation or responding to a message you received. While I don't suggest men compliment women on their photographs to start the conversation, it's not as concerning for a woman to do so.

Not Comfortable Reaching out to Him?

If you are not so sure you want to be the initiator, consider this instead. Simply comment on a guy's profile. Don't worry for a second that you will appear too forward. Guys love flattery!

Use these bullet points to get you started quickly. You will develop your own style once you've done this a few times.

- Send a message about how you enjoyed something in his profile...
- You love his sense of humor, from a story he told.
- Maybe you thought he had great photos.
- Do you share an interest? If you do, mention it here.
- Mention whatever caught your eye. You rarely have to worry about sounding creepy when messaging a man, even if it might seem superficial.

No need to make it long. A few sentences will do and then wish him well. Remember, you are simply complimenting him on something within the profile and mentioning a similarity you might share. You didn't ask him out but you brought the fact that you exist to his attention.

If you are more adventurous, ask an open-ended question to give him something to respond to. With all the profiles, apps, and sites vying for his attention, don't leave it to chance that he might stumble across your profile. Do this and boost your chances! You need not ask him to check your profile or ask him to write back. He will look at your profile, and he will reply if he's interested.

There are guys who want to be the pursuer and won't respond to a woman messaging him. But there are many guys who don't mind getting the A-Okay from a lady who took the time to message him with a compliment. It all comes down to his personality and viewpoint.

Don't Get Caught Up Checking

For both men and women, I suggest you do your online searching as early in the day as you can and seek out three worthy prospects. Message those three and go on with your day. Don't get caught up constantly checking your online dating sites for messages.

You are far more likely to feel anxious and deflated if you are constantly watching for messages. You can set your mobile apps to notify you, so let that tool work for you. Meanwhile use your time to plan other ways to get back out into the social world.

Making the Connection

When you find someone of interest online, the plan should be to meet face-to-face in a reasonably short amount of time. Chatting shouldn't go on for weeks prior to the meeting. If things seem interesting enough to keep talking, then it's time to plan a meeting.

Some people that will have a real charming effect on you have no intention of ever meeting. Some are married and will waste your time playing. If you hit it off online keep moving forward. This will help weed out those who are just playing.

The way online dating works today, you will find that people want to move at a crazy pace. The current swipe right method has made dating apps addicting and heightens the pace at which people expect to move. Guys don't seem bothered by it, but women rarely like the results-oriented rush.

Men are generally looking for speed and results. Guys want to swipe right and meet immediately, from nothing more than a great photo. Ladies are more likely to want to move at a more cautious pace. The highest concern for most women overall is safety and comfort, which it should be.

Where do we go to find a happy medium? If you are a guy, pace it more slowly. She will notice that you aren't moving at the same pace as every other guy is attempting to. It will add a bit of mystery, which is never bad. Remember, we are here for a real, deep relationship. We shouldn't try to follow the same breakneck pace that isn't working to find a deep, meaningful relationship. We want to use the tool, but not at the pace it's being used at by everyone else.

For women, it is important to slow the pace down, but not to a crawl. Your initial plan should be to talk with this person by phone before meeting, not just by text. After ten to fifteen messages back and forth, you can take this meeting offline, and set up a phone call.

A good point at which to move to a phone conversation is once your messaging goes deeper than the initial greetings and small talk. That is a great way to move it off-line. Simply say, "Great question. Why don't you call me and we can talk about it?" This initial phone call should take place within the first week. The phone conversation should give you the basis to decide whether to meet for coffee.

With the ability to communicate in real time in most of today's dating apps, you may be inclined to skip the phone call and communicate through the app right up until you meet. But I really suggest you talk to your potential date by phone before meeting. Texting doesn't count here. There is so much that can't be figured out through the written word. Take the time to learn more about your level of interest from a direct conversation. It's okay to take this in a different route. You are slowing down, and in doing so, building trust. Give your Google phone number, allowing you extra peace of mind, and begin communicating by phone.

Plan to meet over coffee. The great thing about a short first meeting is, neither of you get stuck in a date that lasts for hours with someone you could tell you didn't like within the first twelve seconds of meeting.

Three Reasons to Meet Early On:

1) It will save you from getting into an online romance that will never turn into a face-to-face meeting because the person on the other end isn't serious about meeting you.
2) It keeps you from falling for someone online that you won't like when you meet in person. There is no way an app can create or identify chemistry between people.
3) It will keep you moving forward. It's easier to keep the momentum going than it is to gain it, as chatting online for long periods keeps you from meeting other potential matches.

If you are a woman who has found yourself caught in a conversation online that isn't progressing toward a meeting, just say, "We should get together over coffee and continue this conversation." If he makes no plans still, thank him for his time and wish him the best. If he's legitimately interested, he will set things up. It is common for women who are concerned with appearing too aggressive to get strung along for far too long. Don't let this happen to you. Use online dating as a tool to meet others in person and don't waste time with those who won't. It'll save your heart and your sanity!

It's a Numbers Game

Your goal at this point should be to meet some great prospects. This means meeting a lot of people though. If you feel you have run low on options, reach out to every person you even have slight interest in that doesn't fall outside of your must-haves. If I hadn't taken that extra initiative myself, I would have never met my wife. I reached out to a profile with no photographs, and only a few lines written in her profile. It was only because I hadn't found the right person online already that I even circled back and dove in more deeply to take another look. It was here that I eventually found my wife.

Often people are afraid of being inundated with bad dates if they start reaching out to others who weren't their first choice. If you look for reasons not to contact people on dating sites, you can narrow your scope so far that you find very few people that seem "fitting."

If you only contact the most fitting ones you can easily get discouraged. Low response rates can leave you feeling there is no one out there for you. If your Must-Haves list is covered in your search criteria, be a bit adventurous, and allow yourself to think outside the box. You just may be glad you did.

Getting Hurt

You may get your heart broken online, but you may also get your heart broken in person as well. Not putting all my hope into the next date helped me to recognize that each new meeting was not a life or death situation. Most dates would not render the person I was looking for. When I planned for that up front each date didn't feel like so much was on the line.

A Last Word

This tool we call online dating is the single biggest breakthrough the world has ever seen for meeting people, most of which you would have never run across in life otherwise. You may have heard stories or had a bad previous experience online yourself and are afraid to try again. I have talked to so many who are afraid to try just like I was. But I'm so glad I did. Don't give up on this tool. It is the single largest place to find a future love match!

CHAPTER 16
ACTING AND THINKING CONFIDENTLY

"Sometimes the only way to get a quality in reality is to start behaving as if you have it already."- C.S. Lewis

You may feel your lack of confidence is visible to everyone you meet. Understanding what gives you the appearance of confidence can change that game entirely. As you build your confidence, let's work on giving you a confident look. In other words, fake it till you make it.

True confidence in anything comes only after becoming competent in it. But acting confident can positively alter your frame of mind until you get there. Acting confident even when you are sweating it out puts you in a position where you can grow both your competence and confidence.

Don't get "acting" confident confused with trying to act like someone you are not. I am simply portraying confidence. I recognized the company I keep can sway my confidence. So can how I choose to spend my time, how I feel that day, the way I dress, and the decisions I make.

As I got back out there, I never pretended to have a lot of money, I didn't lie about my age, or anything else for that matter. I simply smiled, spoke first, shook hands, greeted others, and asked them questions about themselves.

I was still being myself, but just being a more self-assured version of me. When I refer to "acting confident," it's about learning to look calm, cool, and collected even when you are not feeling that way. It is a part you will find allows you to enjoy life more and allows you to grow as a person. So, how do you get there?

Getting Started

Start by reminding yourself of the great qualities you have by looking back at the list you created in the companion course exercise. Go a step further by making a copy of this and place it in a location where you can regularly see it. Another option is to post it in your mobile device so you can bring it up at will. Use it as a reminder to yourself of the value you bring to others around you. It is easy to forget your great qualities and dwell on your "negatives" when you try something new.

Preparation

Place sticky notes around your home that say, "Do it with confidence" or "Confidence, Confidence, Confidence." Put them in conspicuous areas such as a bathroom mirror or your vehicle's dashboard or inside of the front door. This can be useful just before an event to remind yourself to think confidently, or as a motivator throughout the day.

Look your best. Be prepared by showering, shaving, makeup, and your nails. It is amazing what a little teeth whitening will do to improve appearance. Dress the part of confidence. What clothing have you gotten the most compliments in? When you dress your best, you feel stronger. See yourself dressing the part of a confident person in a movie. This is your dress rehearsal for a more confident you.

Practice walking *as if* self-assured. Shoulders back, with upright posture. Now walk as you normally do. Notice the difference in how you carry yourself? Do this at home now, but practice when you are out in public too. Just becoming aware is a huge first step.

Set yourself up for success by listening to a preset playlist of songs that inspires and encourages you. Do this while getting ready, and while traveling to your destination. Music really changes our state, and it's a great jumpstart when your confidence needs a boost.

Smiling and Eye Contact

Smiling makes you look confident and unafraid, which makes it easier for others to talk to you. This is the single biggest step you can take to become more approachable. If you feel others don't try to connect with you, your lack of smile or eye contact could be the problem.

This is the single biggest step I took in breaking out of my lack of self-confidence. If you need to do more of this, it's likely you've already heard this from friends, family and coworkers.

Look people in the eye when you smile at them. Confident people don't look down when approaching others. I still to this day catch myself with this one. When I do, I remind myself to bring my eyes up off the floor. If you struggle with this, begin by looking older people in the eye and smiling. Doing so will give you practice and can brighten someone else's day at the same time. If you do this enough, you can graduate to speaking to them. All this is good prep work for your more confident future.

Speak First

Greeting others instead of waiting for them to speak first afforded me the largest boost in my confidence, as it allowed me to take a proactive lead role in my behavior toward others. What I quickly learned was when I took this approach, others saw me as confident and a leader even when I was anything but. Their assertion that I was a confident person boosted my confidence and allowed me to become just that.

Speak to others without waiting for them to speak first. Self-assured people are proactive in reaching out to others. Many times, I've heard a shy person say, "He didn't even speak to me." The key is that this person was being reactive by waiting for others to start conversation... This gives all your power to the other person. You are waiting for them to say hello, and they are likely waiting for you, wondering why you aren't speaking to them. It's time to become proactive.

Playing the part of being confident doesn't entail acting snooty, being loud and boisterous, or putting others down. It's a good chance those actions are shown by someone attempting to appear confident and in control. It has been my observation that confident people are often gracious, aware of the feelings of others, thankful, and kind. Being warm and kind will set you apart from others instantly. It will naturally draw others to want to be around you. You will show confidence while growing your confidence.

Taking Action

Another important thing to consider in the appearance of confidence is in showing boldness by taking action and stepping up to make or offer plans. If this is an area of weakness for you, begin practicing this with family and business opportunities. Suggest plans, offer restaurants, and be the first to take that action. This shows confidence and boldness.

This was a learning experience for me, as I'm easygoing. I prefer to let others have a say in decisions. Still, I learned I had to take these actions because that was often what my date was expecting me to do. Have suggestions at the ready so you can offer up a great coffee shop, restaurant, or activity when the need arises.

Things to Consider

- Confidence is a mindset.
- People you encounter have no idea if you are confident or not, except by the actions you display. If you look and sound confident, others naturally assume you are.
- Remember, the world is responding to how you act, not how you feel.

Ever try something you weren't excited about, only to find it was easy after you gave it a chance? That's what "fake it till you make it" can do for you. It gives you the platform on which to build your confidence.

Things to Keep in Mind as You Move Forward

When you get back out there, doing the following things will give others the impression that you are a warm, confident person, even when you are scared.

- Smile
- Greet others first
- Shake hands
- Ask questions about them.

CHAPTER 17
WE ALL HAVE THE SAME FEAR

"I have lived a long life and had many troubles, most of which never happened."
- Mark Twain

As we get ready to create a new social life, you may be excited and a bit nervous, or you may be wondering if you can even take the next step. I'm here to tell you that you can. You can thank me for it later. While these fears are stirring around in your head, I want to let you in on a secret. One thing that has been consistently amazing to me is that we all have the same fears.

Men and women alike share the need to belong, feel accepted, and feel valued. I've consistently heard both men and women say the same thing, though they use different words to describe it. Deep inside, each one of us is afraid we are not enough. We don't really want anyone else to know that we feel this way about ourselves, and we often think these feelings are unique to us. So we keep quiet.

When I am one-on-one with nearly anyone, and I have allowed myself to be vulnerable, I have been amazed that even those men and women who appear most confident will share these feelings of inadequacy in an environment that allows it. In any other environment however, we all want to appear to that we have it all together.

Have you ever seen someone you wanted to go talk to, but ended up walking away without so much as a word? All of us have been there, and that scenario happened to me many times. There was always that little voice chiming in that was saying "You aren't good enough."

Recognizing that others around me felt the same, despite what they outwardly showed made a world of difference in my perspective. It showed me that feeling this way at times meant that I was perfectly normal. It does not matter how good-looking someone is either. I have found that the prettiest people are often just as insecure as the rest of us. It's easy to get caught up spending far too much time focusing on what is wrong with me, and not enough on what is great about who God made me.

Am I Good Enough?

When my confidence is low, it is easy to for me to see that I am not "good enough" in who I am and what I have to offer. Simply taking a different perspective on the same situation and attaching significance to who I am lets me see things in a whole new light.

For instance, if I feel little value in myself, I can't see why anyone would want to be with me. This thought process will keep me from making the effort. I'll go out less, pursue less often, and create a self-fulfilling prophecy.

None of us like rejection, but when I see my own value it is easier to shift my thoughts back to a positive frame when I face it.

Reaching out to make connections and serving the needs of others in the community is just one way to remind myself of the value and significance I have in the lives of others. This helps me reframe my thoughts that can help me bridge tough moments.

Not only does it give me purpose and hope, but others see it as well. My confidence in that area of life is felt by others around me in those scenarios. People naturally gravitate to those who serve with confidence, which is another positive effect of finding value in who you are.

But I Just Can't…

Since it's difficult for you to grow beyond the image of who you think you are, it is important to find value in yourself. You can start changing those beliefs by changing the questions you ask yourself, and the way you choose to answer. Henry Ford once said, "Whether you think you can, or you think you can't, you're right."

The first step in changing my words involves how you take away your own ability simply by saying so. We all have something we say we "can't do," whether it be going to a crowded party, dancing, starting a conversation with a stranger, or asking someone for a date. When I say that I can't do something, I take away the possibility of it altogether.

Statements like "I just can't talk to people, be nice, dance, meet new people, go to parties. I can't lose weight, smile, speak in front of a group" are all examples of this. You can fill in the blanks. While this is a course specifically in dating confidence, each of us comes to it with our own fears and concerns.

When I say I can't do something, I'm really stating that I don't have confidence in my ability to make it happen, or that the anxiety that arises just from the consideration of it feels overwhelming. If I say it often enough, I build a cage of excuses around myself that keeps me from facing that fear.

How do we get out of the trap? Do it. It's as simple as that. It may not be easy, but the solution is simple. Face it in little steps if needed but face it. It's always a matter of deciding to take the risk.

What have you said, "I can't do" that involves meeting people, dating, and other social interactions?

Some of My Concerns Were:

- Attending a Meetup group where I didn't know anyone.
- Dancing in public
- Asking someone out

In truth, at some point I think I'd said, "I can't" to just about everything I did in this book.

Consider What Some of Yours may Be:

- What is one thing you want to conquer?
- What is the very first thing you need to do to conquer it?
- What might I gain by accomplishing this?
- What is the worst thing that could happen?
- What would happen to me if that worst-case scenario occurred?

Often, just writing down the fear, and seeing it logically helps. Weighing out the possible scenarios, good and bad, can help you see that your fear isn't a life or death situation. It can also help you see it from an entirely different perspective, outside of all the fear and emotion you've always tied to it.

In the movie "Back to the Future," Marty McFly realizes how tiny decisions are affecting his whole life, as he sees how his life would have been different by making alternative choices. The mad scientist, Dr. Emmett Brown warns that the slightest incidents while he is time traveling could change the entire course of human history.

It's just a movie, but if you've seen it, it gives a great visual illustration of how a slight event shift now can alter your very real life later. In a very real sense, that's what you have the opportunity to do. While you can't go back in time, you can redirect the course you are on, and change your future forever.

Any decision you make, including doing nothing at all, affects your future. You are writing the script to your life, and the decisions you make, one by one, affect the script. Are you ready to start rewriting yours?

CHAPTER 18
STEPPING BACK OUT INTO A SOCIAL WORLD

"Forget past mistakes. Forget failures. Forget everything except what you are going to do now and do it." - William Durant

Do you remember the first time you drove a car? I think it's safe to say that it was intimidating. Check your mirrors, watch the speed limit, and navigate the yield lanes. "Did I remember to use my turn signals?" It was scary at first, and it all felt overwhelming, with far too many things to remember at once.

As I learned each of the steps, I began to relax. Slowly it became second nature. Is it any wonder that almost everyone drives? We wouldn't have thought of getting in the car, driving the first few blocks, and then parking it and exclaiming, "Forget it! I'll never learn to drive!" This is what so many of us do to ourselves in the dating world. Before we've even given ourselves time to get comfortable and familiar to the process, we drop out, and spend Friday nights watching TV with our cat.

Decide to start. You could spend months or years contemplating the next move or pick it and start. I'm here to tell you that the start is the hardest part, but the part that brings all the success. Will you make mistakes along the way? You certainly will, but you will learn and grow.

In the business world, you plan and then you execute. Then you take what you learned, tweak the plan, and execute. That's exactly what you will do here.

The Amazing Value of Meetup Groups

When I got started, I thought online dating would be enough. Many singles use this as their sole means of meeting new people. But for me, I couldn't stand sitting behind my phone waiting to find people online. Plus, I realized I needed to brush up on my social skills. I decided quickly I needed to do more. In addition, I was determined to employ as many methods as possible to meet the right person.

It was time for me to find ways to meet people in social situations. I needed a way to increase the number of people I met. But I had no intention of ending up in a bar to meet someone. Since I don't drink alcohol anyway, the idea of me sipping a fountain drink at the local pub made it even worse. I also realize this wasn't the place to meet the kind of person I was looking for anyway. Like so many others I've talked to in this same situation, however, it was the first picture of dating I could conjure up.

One evening while sitting home pondering my next step, I searched online for "Best ways to meet people in Fredericksburg, Virginia.". I kept coming across something called Meetups. I was completely unaware of what it was but became intrigued when any Google search for "meeting people" ended with this same result.

What I found was that Meetup is an online social networking service where you can go to join groups of people who have similar interests to yours. While this isn't a "singles only" community, there are many singles groups within, and plenty of singles who take part in other groups too. Anyone can set up a book club, or a mom's group. There are hiker's groups, running groups, recovery groups, board game groups, dancing clubs, singles groups. The list is incredible. Many are free, or nearly free.

To find out more, go to meetup.com, or download the app. Once there, choose from a list of interests, and search for groups based on zip code. You can set a parameter of distance from the zip code you enter. If you are in a rural area, you can increase the distance you are willing to travel to find groups of interest.

Depending on where you live, you may see some singles Meetups with thousands of members. Don't let that intimidate you. Some people sign up, but rarely attend. Our lives are busy, and we don't all follow through with the things we set out to do. Also, many who join singles groups never get around to removing themselves from this list. What is important is how many members are actively involved. You will find that out by seeing how many people regularly attend events (which you can do once you have become a group member).

If you live in a rural area, you may find just one or two groups. In other areas, you may find dozens. Take advantage of what is there. If you are willing to travel a bit, you are likely to find active singles Meetups in your nearest large town.

Once I setup my profile, and joined a group, I could then see the other individual members profiles within that group. There were multiple singles groups listed in my area. Most singles groups were set up with age ranges, so I joined all the groups I could.

I felt my first rush of optimism! I knew this was a way I could expand myself socially and get to meet new people. Singles group events are planned for people to get out of the house, have a good time, get to know others, and maybe, just maybe, find the right someone.

Often if there is a local event going on, such as a festival, the Meetup organizer can schedule to have a group meet for that event. In these instances, you will have group members plus others from outside of the group in attendance.

Anytime I had a free night on my upcoming schedule, I could check for events that were happening. This got me out of the house regularly, allowed me to hone my social skills, and gave me a sense of hope that anytime I went, I never knew who I might get to meet. Suddenly I had a calendar of events to add to my schedule. Also, because most of the groups I first gravitated to were singles groups, I knew that those attending were also single, and likely were there for the same reasons as I was.

When an event is set members of that group RSVP if they wish to attend. The RSVP list provides good insight on how many people plan to attend the event. If there were multiple events going on the same night, I could choose the one that seemed the most fun, cost the least, or the one with the most people going. It was not uncommon to arrive at a planned event only to meet someone who had just moved into town and didn't know anyone. They often showed up without appearing on the RSVP list either. I met interesting people this way regularly, that I never expected to see, based on the "attendees" list.

You may be saying to yourself, "I'm not signing up. I wouldn't know what to do or say at these events. This whole social thing seems way too intimidating." If that is you, don't worry. We will cover that shortly. For now, set stop reading and go check out Meetups. Sign up for the singles groups in your area that are a fit for you.

Getting Started

The first event I signed up for was at a restaurant in town. It was a dinner get together, and I made sure I arrived early. I ate before I went, only ordering a small appetizer while I was there, and spent my time bouncing between open seats to introduce myself and talk to as many people as possible, both men and women. It was out of my comfort zone, but I was going to take massive action, and this was the best way I saw to do it.

One important tip I found; arrive early whenever possible. This allowed me to pick and choose who I sat near. It also set me up to greet others when they arrived. I found that welcoming others, as opposed to being welcomed by a sea of faces, gave me much more sense of control and confidence.

Those who arrive late (especially first timers, and those who don't attend regularly) will see you as a warm, kind, and welcoming member, and will sense that you are in control. It's an interesting concept, but it works.

My goal that evening was to meet as many people as possible, Staying in one place all night would have been far more comfortable, but I knew I had to come out of my shell, and I wanted that night to be the start of it.

Did I meet a love interest that night? No, I didn't. I could have decided that first Meetup was a waste of my time. I didn't though. I knew I was on the right track to building my confidence and social skills. I did meet other people in the same boat as myself. I also met my friend, Carolyn that evening. Later on, she plays a critical role in helping me past my fear of dancing. But that is a different story.

I am thankful this first event went well for me and had good attendance. Having a negative experience at this event may have left me with a very different first impression, and a very different outlook. Remember that each experience and event is unique. Don't throw in the towel if your first experience isn't all that you had hoped for.

Don't get tied up in the idea that you have to meet the right person each time you go out. Instead, use these opportunities to hone your social skills, so that when you do meet someone that interests you, you will have gotten some rookie mistakes out of the way.

Over time, I attended Meetup events that had as few as 5 members show up, and others where there were 75 members. Your first event might not be well attended, or have anyone you have any interest in. But don't let that keep you from going back or checking into additional groups to add to your list. Small towns will likely have fewer attendees, but these are still powerful places to get to know others, get comfortable, and increase your competence.

Build Relationships

It's been my experience that in these groups, people truly seek friendships and camaraderie. When you take the time to get to know everyone in the group, and build relationships, those members are likely to speak highly of you when another member shows an interest in you. I was amazed at this process, but it did seem to be the case in group after group. Besides, when does building friendships ever hurt? You may be thinking "I am going to these to meet a future partner, not to find friendships." You are indeed. That's the reason most people get into a singles group to begin with. But the other members can help you in your quest or hinder you based on the way you treat them. It's your choice.

You may be thinking "I can't afford to go out and attend these events on my budget." I felt the same way when I first investigated Meetups. But I found that if I was a bit creative, I could attend many of the events with very little out of pocket cost.

If the group was meeting at a restaurant, I would often eat a meal at home before attending and grab just a drink or an appetizer at the restaurant. At first, I was very self-conscious of this, but I quickly realized that no one else cared. In time, I realized others were finding their own creative ways to get out and still stay within their own budget. Once I became comfortable, there were times I would order a water and socialize. It gave me more time to focus on building relationships, which was my aim anyway.

If the group went out for an event such as bowling, I could pay and play, or just come by for social time. Once I had spent my allotted budget for going out for that month, I chose to attend the events that didn't have a cost associated with them. Do not let budgetary issues keep you from getting started. Get creative in your thinking and planning, and you can spend less while getting the full benefit of the groups.

You may be thinking, "This method is going to take too long." It likely will take time, but the goal is to continue to expand your world. As a single person trying to figure this out, you've probably experienced the feeling that "There isn't anyone out there for me."

It is Easy to React One of Two Ways When You Feel There is no One

1) You stop trying altogether.

2) You settle for someone that isn't a good match because they are physically present because you hate dating, and you have lost hope of finding a great match.

These are perfectly normal feelings, and you will feel that way from time to time. Every step you are taking is there to expand your world and minimize the number of times you feel this way. Meetup groups are yet another way to expand your circle of connections.

Meetup Groups (singles Meetups in particular) will help you:

- Fill up lonely spots in your calendar.
- Get back out and socialize in small groups.
- Learn the art of small talk
- Have fun with other people you have things in common with.
- Get practice having deep conversations with people.
- Make new single friends.
- Flirt (when the time is right).
- Go out on dates.
- Possibly meet a soulmate.

What I Learned from Meetup Groups

- There are all kinds of people that attend Meetups. This isn't just for the "in crowd" (whatever that is). People of all ages, shapes and sizes, and walks of life attend. That mix varies with every group.
- I could use the RSVP list to get at least a good idea of who was going to an event. Not everyone signs up, and an RSVP isn't a guarantee of who will show up. It is a starting point though.
- I signed up early for events. Remember, not only are you looking to see who is going, others may be looking to see if you are going!
- I learned to sign up for both large and small events. Smaller groups can mean more intimate conversation. And new people that just joined your group could show up any time.
- There are people in every walk of life who are natural matchmakers. In small community groups such as Meetups, the matchmakers will often help you get connected with others.
- I would have thought singles groups would have been a dog-eat-dog world. Instead, I found small communities where people were looking to connect with other human beings.

- I built friendships with both men and women in the groups I was in, which I didn't initially expect.
- I learned to greet newcomers to the group which gave them the impression that I was self-assured and confident, even when I wasn't.
- I didn't come on too strong or too fast to new people who I might be interested in getting to know. I would introduce myself and be careful to not be overbearing.
- Meetup groups gave me a chance to hone my conversation skills with others of the opposite sex in a low-pressure situation, before I was out on a date, and the stakes were higher.
- Singles groups were the only groups where it is expected that the person you are interested in getting to know is not married. This is a great reason to sign up for as many singles groups as possible.
- If you are willing to travel to the next town over, you will find other singles groups as well.

As big as Meetups are, I am surprised how few singles know about them. They are a nice "hidden gem" that shouldn't be overlooked!

Just the Beginning

Don't stop at singles Meetups groups though. Do you like to hike? Are you into photography? Do you want to learn the art of public speaking? Join a dance group? How about a beer drinkers book club?

Get warmed up with the singles groups, because it is a good start socially, and you can easily tell who is single. Expand yourself (and your social network) by joining other groups. It's a great way to get out of the house more. Plus, when you join other special interest groups, you spend time with people who you share like-minded enthusiasm with. It's much easier to start and keep a conversation going when you share an interest.

We need to nurture the relationships and interests we have in life that will naturally make us more interesting on a date. Having a healthy life and social life make us more interesting to the opposite sex. You become a better partner to others. No one wants to go out with someone who has no life outside of sitting in their apartment, swiping right all day.

We each want to find someone who is motivated, optimistic, enthusiastic, makes us laugh, and has a plan. Looking from the other person's perspective, does this describe me? This isn't just about fixing my love life, but about creating a more dynamic life. If you work to improve your own quality of life, you will naturally create better relationships, be happier and more optimistic. This will organically attract people searching for the more dynamic person you are becoming.

We should use all the tools given to us. We should always look at the whole. The improvements you make here will change your interactions with everyone you meet. You will find your friendships and coworker relationships grow naturally in this process. In addition, science shows that most of us will meet and marry someone through a social network. This is a valid reason to become more social.

Steps to Take Today to Get Involved:

- Go to www.meetup.com or download the app.
- Scroll through the myriad of groups available in or around your area.
- Click on several groups of interest and sign up. The more you sign up for the more choices you will have to fill your calendar.
- Add a head and shoulder photo of you. Choose an image that is not being used on a dating site or is elsewhere on the web.

The enrollment process is easy. You will usually have to answer a few questions, and then the organizer will grant you permission to join.

Once you've joined groups of interest to you, check their calendar of upcoming events. Choose an event to sign up for and get this ball rolling. You may be hesitant, but this is the surest way to victory. Plan it, push past your fear, and read on!

CHAPTER 19
PLANNING YOUR FIRST MEETUP

"Attitude is the difference between an ordeal and an adventure" - Anonymous

Now that you have some dates on your calendar, don't let yourself pause. Whatever event you plan to attend, recognize you will be nervous. This isn't an excuse not to show up, or not to socialize though. It's the normal thing we all feel, and it is part of what makes us human. You may be thinking, "But what about the magic formula to help me get over my lack of confidence?" That's what this step is all about. The theory, therapists and self-help books are no help until you get out there and start. Taking action is where the change begins.

Preplanning

Plan ahead with a few questions you can ask people you meet at your first Meetup. Having nothing to say can keep you from talking to anyone. If you have a few things to ask, however, you can let them do the talking.

Don't concern yourself if it feels like trivial conversation. Really intelligent people sometimes feel like small talk is a waste of time. But normal conversation patterns for people meeting for the first time involve small talk. It's just how conversations start. You can't meet someone for the first time and lead with earth-shattering questions, you will find people trying to get away as quickly as possible.

Light questions on light topics are how we get to know one another. The deeper questions can come once you've established a bit of rapport. Have a few questions memorized that allow you to seem confident and curious. It can start with something as simple as "Where are you from?"

Set Yourself Up for Success

Did you set a goal for tonight? Set goals for social outings before you ever head out. Goals should start off as something to the effect of "I intend to get to know three new people tonight." At each successive event, step up your goal a bit. Now you have a plan which you can work toward and feel good about at the end of the evening. Give yourself credit for meeting your goal and see yourself placing another brick in the foundation.

Too often, our plan is to meet our next relationship. While it could happen, and it is the overall aim, these goals leave you feeling worse at the end of the evening when you go home without having met them. Or worse, they lead you to make a connection you might not have otherwise, just to meet your criteria of a successful night out.

Set objectives to each outing that stretch you and give you competence in this game. Give yourself a reasonably achievable goal that stretches you out of your comfort zone but doesn't set you up for poor decision making.

Arrive Prepared

Be prepared when you arrive, so you can simply get out of the car and go in without hesitation. The longer you take to get out of the car, the more likely you will be to turn around and go back home. Many times, men and women have told me they arrived, only to mull it over in the parking lot. Then they ended up back home because they gave themselves time to think about it. Don't give yourself time to back out.

The Event

Once inside, plan to move around, and not get locked into just one location, or one group of people. Becoming a wallflower at any event makes you feel even more insecure. Moving around will help use up some of your nervous energy. This energy can make you feel shaky, adding to the nervousness itself. Any physical activity at all can help reduce the extra "fight or flight" energy.

Another plus of moving around is that, to the onlooker, you appear to be confidently mingling. Many of those attending will stick with an area that makes them most comfortable. Your movement increases the likelihood of making connections with far more people, most just as nervous as you.

The more self-conscious you are, the more you feel all eyes are on you. Everyone else is worried about how they appear to those around them. Each person there is too wrapped up in themselves to know you feel the jitters. Remember this when you are sure everyone is watching!

It is far easier to walk in and speak to people as you come in contact with them than to come in silent and try to figure out how to speak to them later. Most of the people in the room are just like you. They know only a few people at most, and by you taking the time to greet them warmly, you are now the magnet in the room. You take on the role of the friendly, confident one.

Your greeting can open doors you wouldn't believe. Opening your shy personality up so the world can get to know you will change how others perceive you, and this will change how you perceive you, in more ways than you can even imagine!

Your personality and experiences have shaped you over a lifetime. It is important to realize that even with effort, it will take time to structure your confidence, so be patient with yourself, especially if you tend to have perfectionist tendencies. Always look at each step you take as a victory.

What am I Telling Others?

What you say is only a small part of the equation. One of the most common questions I get is "What should I say?" Did you know that what you say only makes up about 20 percent of the first impression you make? Yet this is the part we are all worried about.

Here's how experts Allan and Barbara Pease say it roughly breaks down:

- •55% nonverbal cues or body language.
- •38% our voice inflection, or the way we say things.
- •7% the actual words we use.

Your body language gives strong visual clues of who you are, and what you think of those you meet. You translate these messages to the world through your facial expressions, movements and gestures. People put more stock in what your body language "says" than in the actual words you speak. So it is important to become aware of your mannerisms, and how they affect others impression of you. Learning to make subtle changes can make a big difference.

A Smile is Worth a Thousand Words (or at Least the First Hundred)

During a photoshoot at my studio, I overheard heard a client of mine tell her daughter, "A smile is the best makeup ever!" Your smile or lack of it, paints a picture of you to the rest of the world that says either "I'm open and friendly" or "leave me to myself." As difficult as it may be for you to see, an outsider can often spot it from a mile away. To add to it, if that outsider mentioned it to you, it would likely make you defensive. That's a good way to know it was probably accurate.

If you are shy, it's easy for your lack of smile and quiet nature to appear arrogant or aloof to the outside world. Your discomfort in a social situation may be read as "uncaring and unapproachable." If you wonder why people don't talk with you much at social gatherings, this may be the reason.

People around you form an opinion based on the information you are subconsciously sharing with them. Are you painting the picture of a warm, kind, approachable person? Smiling more than you might be comfortable with, along with saying, "Hello" will change others' perception of you, and open new doors. It will make others more comfortable in approaching you, too, which can lead to all kinds of good things.

As I mentioned earlier, I was once incredibly shy. I overanalyzed everything I did or considered doing. The problem is, that stifled me from doing anything. What I've found is the more uncomfortable I am with doing this, the more I needed to do it! If you can't bear the thought of it, start by smiling more often than you are comfortable with. You don't have to tackle it all in one day, but it is time to move in the right direction.

When you are overly concerned about what to do, it keeps you from reacting at all, even in simple things such as expressions. Your face is saying, "Leave me alone," when it is often the last thing you really want.

Maintain Eye Contact

Maintaining eye contact lets others know you are interested in what they are saying. Don't let your eyes wander around the room when someone is talking to you. It gives the appearance of being disinterested. Give the person who is talking your full attention. If you are doing the talking, be sure to look at the person you are talking to. People are more willing to trust you when you can look them in the eye during a conversation.

All this takes practice and won't feel natural to you. You will find your eyes wandering off, and when you do, bring them back to the person you are talking with. Don't beat yourself up. It's a learning process. Let yourself grow and give yourself a break.

Put Your Phone Away

I admit I struggled with this one and still do. Just like the rest of us, I've grown used to my phone providing ready-made entertainment, and filling every moment of dead space in my day. The problem is, you can only reach out (or be reached by others) in that same dead space you are trying to fill by using the phone.

People are more likely to reach out to you when you aren't tied up in the middle of something else. When your attention is turned toward your phone, you are not as reachable.

I began to realize that, while my phone comforted me in uncomfortable situations, it kept me from seeking out the company of others. It also told the world I was too preoccupied with something else for them to waste their time.

In social situations, our phones can pull us away from uncomfortable moments, allowing us to not experience them. In doing so, they are stunting our ability to communicate in personal situations.

Lack of a smile, keeping to yourself, and playing on your phone while others talk paints a picture of someone who doesn't want to be bothered. You miss so much when your attention is directed toward your device instead of the rest of the world. These days, use of your phone counts as body language.

Gratitude

If someone holds a door for you, be sure to always look them in the eye, say thank you, and smile. I've seen over and again people that let their quietness keep them from showing appreciation for others for what they have done for them. But to the giver, it comes off as rude. This certainly isn't reserved for just the shy, as so many people today seem ungrateful to small acts of kindness from strangers.

Looking Back on My Early Meetups

After attending my first Meetup, I could see great value in them, so I signed up for three more singles groups. I began to fill my calendar with things to get me out of the house. My social skills were rusty, but I found this to be a good place to practice and improve them.

After attending my third event, I'd set my eyes on Susan, the organizer of one of the singles groups. I'd met her previously, and she seemed to be a sweet person. I thought she would say yes if I asked her out. It didn't work out that way.

I asked her one evening after a Meetup if she'd like to go out with me. "No," she said. "I am only in the group to get out of the house. I'm not interested in dating right now." I was crushed on my first attempt.

A couple nights later, I awkwardly attended another Meetup event with the same group. One of the ladies, unaware that I had asked her out, mentioned a Facebook post of Susan's from the day before. "How come the only men interested in me aren't the least bit interesting," recapped the other member, regarding Susan's post. "Wow," I thought. That statement seemed to point right at me!

My first attempt at getting up on the horse left me on the ground with the wind knocked out of me. I could have stopped there. I thought about it. Many people stop there. Know ahead that setbacks will happen to you many times. Determine ahead of time that it won't stop you when it does. There is a reason it doesn't work out.

There will be times when you will be on the other end of it, and you will turn down the advances of someone who is interested in you. They will be the one getting hurt. When it happens to you, don't take it personally. Just thank them and move forward. Easy to say, I know. But it's the only way to move from where you are to where you want to be.

The groups I became involved with scheduled a variety of activities. After-work Meetups for dinner were not uncommon. But other events included winery tours, Friday night dances, meeting up for drinks, Karaoke night, hikes, pool parties, and backyard cookouts, to name a few.

Each event provided unique opportunities to meet new people, get to know the regulars, and touch up my conversational skills. It is through these that I met lifelong friends that I still correspond with.

At Meetups, I was relearning how to interact with people of the opposite sex as if it were a dress rehearsal for dating. I found I could also observe others I might have an interest in from a slight distance.

Here are Just a few Things I could Learn from Observation:

- Do they drink too much?
- Are they kind and thoughtful?
- Loud and outrageous?
- Are they annoying?

- Flirty with everyone?
- What do they talk about?
- How do they treat others?
- Do I like their personality?
- Do we have common interests?

These and many other questions I could answer before I ever asked them out. And asked them out I did! I found most ladies were supportive of one another in the groups. I could see them play Cupid at times, and because I was kind to everyone in my group, they would put in a good word for me with new people in the group. This really helps, as many single people have negative past experiences, and are hesitant to jump in again with both feet. Having others in the group suggesting you as a good catch helps. I can't guarantee those results in every group, but this was my experience.

The same basic tips work whether you are taking a class, going to a singles event, or sitting at a wedding reception. Showing kindness to others, saying hello, and looking people in the eye with a warm smile are all universal ways to open yourself to a world of people.

A Note About Fear

The thought of going out and socializing at your first Meetup may feel overwhelming. Your heart races, the adrenaline is pumping, and you break out in a sweat...and that's while you are still at home thinking about it! It doesn't have to feel that way forever though.

Military, police, firefighters and other first responders train to operate and respond appropriately in the face of great stress and danger. When those men and women go into training for the first time, most will have heart rates at a level that impairs their ability to function fully. Each time they rehearse those same drills, however, their heart rate lowers. Each time they respond better than the last.

The same will happen to you. Each time you accept the challenge you will find your anxiety level a bit lower, and your comfort level a little higher. Each time that happens your confidence grows.

CHAPTER 20
BREAKING THE ICE

"Everything you ever wanted is on the other side of fear." - George Addair

We all want the magic words that break the ice and give us the best chance of opening the doors to a positive interaction. Truth is, the only magic words are those that get said. In the fear of saying the wrong thing, often nothing gets said at all. But saying nothing is a complete and utter roadblock to positive interaction.

Ice breakers and small talk can sometimes feel trivial, disingenuous, and a waste of time. Yet people do business with, become friends with, date, and fall in love with those they know, like, and trust. A great way to accomplish this is to be able to open conversations confidently.

If you've found this tough in the past, it will feel difficult at first, but don't give up. Any small talk you open with is light years ahead of keeping quiet. Having several pre-planned thoughts for icebreakers will give you a springboard from which to dive into a conversation.

You employ icebreakers the same way no matter the situation; opening a conversation at a Meetup, coffee shop, or a business meeting. This makes ice-breaking a powerful tool in building friendships, business relations, or finding a date.

Those Who are Good at Conversation:

- Show a genuine interest in the others.
- Put others at ease.

- Are good, active listeners.
- Don't have an agenda.

Two important Things to Consider:

- Nearly anything you say is more effective than saying nothing at all. It's not as much the words you say as it is how you say them.

Don't hesitate. If you give yourself time to think about it, you are more likely not to speak.

Guys-What Not to Say

Leave out any kind of cat calls or sexually charged comments. This might have worked when you were a teenager to get a female's attention. And yes, you have seen it work in the movies. But that's the same place you saw E.T. fly overhead with an entourage of kids on bicycles too. Did you believe that?

It's been my observation that guys often use catcalls and dumb pick-up lines when they are in the presence of other guys. The quickest way to look juvenile is to employ these techniques. It doesn't show confidence, instead it implies immaturity. Catcalls won't stack the odds in your favor.

The plan here is to meet adults who enjoy other adults, who could make good long-term suitors. It is not to find one of the few desperately in need of a surface compliment or catcall. Yet I understand that the guy who needs to hear this most is the least likely to be reading this.

As I was putting on the finishing touches to this book, I was in a conversation with a group of guys regarding meeting women. One man, who is my age says, "Well how are you going to know she likes you unless you say something inappropriate to her?" At least I know this is a point that some of us still need reminding of!

Steps to Breaking the Ice

There are many great ways to break into a conversation. One simple, yet powerful icebreaker is to simply walk up and ask, "How are you doing?" Then extend your hand for a handshake and give the other person your name. Remember to listen for their name. This bold approach may seem hard to do, but it's a simple approach, and it has confidence written all over it.

Keep the Conversation Going

- What is relevant to your current situation? Is it the smell of coffee at a coffee shop? Whatever best applies to the situation at hand will sound authentic.
- Comment on traffic issues getting there. "I left early and still got here late. Was traffic bad for you?"
- Ask how they know the host of the party or event.
- Comment on a local event. Are they are planning to attend it?
- Comment on a newsworthy happening.
- Talk about the weather. Can you believe this weather we are having?
- Guys-While you can comment on current sports headlines, if she isn't interested in sports, it's a quick way to end the conversation. Save it for the lady who is wearing sports paraphernalia.
- "I love this song. It's always been a favorite of mine. How about you?"
- Compliment an item they are wearing. It is much safer to comment on her shoes, than to compliment her directly on her good looks. I used this many times and never once got a negative look.
- Ask for suggestions-a place to find an item, or a good place to eat nearby.
- Comment on or ask a question on the other person's choice of food or drink.
- Make an observation about something you both just witnessed but avoid making a disparaging comment about another person.
- Talk about a movie. "Have you seen ______________? If your acquaintance says "yes," you have something to talk about. If the answer is "no," ask what type movies they like.

I suggest you choose three of these (or make up your own) that seem comfortable for you. Memorize them and use them repeatedly until you are comfortable with them. Don't go into brain overload trying to remember them all though. You can come up with others after you build confidence in using this simple technique. As stated before, the words are less important than taking the action to step out of your comfort zone.

Things to Consider:

- Don't mention a woman's beauty. I've seen guys compliment a lady on her beauty or sexiness, only to have her instantly get creeped out, and want to disappear.

- Keep any opener positive. It's easy when you are nervous, to let a small negative turn into a rant. Keep it positive!

One great way to break the ice is to become an organizer of a group. The organizer is the front line to meet new people, and they are the one people turn to when they have questions. This works as a natural icebreaker.

Understand that at a core level, men and women want the same things in life; to be accepted for who they are, to be loved, and to have a sense of purpose in their lives. Guys and ladies often express it differently, but we are seeking those same things whether or not we recognize it. When you take this into consideration, it's less about the slick words, and far more about connecting.

Are ice breakers foolproof? Nothing ever is. While most of the world wants to connect, some prefer to be left alone to their thoughts. Recognize this and don't take it as a personal insult if they don't respond in a way you would like. Just say, "Have a great day" and move on. What's the positive in this? If a person doesn't want to converse, and they let you know, they saved you from wasting your valuable time on them. Find the positive in the situation, and you can bounce back more quickly.

Practicing your conversation skills in everyday situations will allow your confidence to grow. This will be inflected in your voice, and the way you handle yourself. Rehearse your opening lines and conversations ahead of time with a friend or in the mirror, so you go in with competence. Having simple, easy to remember techniques makes the first step so much easier!

Have you heard the old story about the two guys who were being chased by a bear, and one stopped to tie his shoes? His friend asked, "What the heck are you doing? You can't outrun that bear! I don't need to outrun the bear, he replied. I just need to outrun you!" Icebreakers are like lacing up your shoes so you can outrun the others in the room, even by just a little.

CHAPTER 21
APPROACH ANXIETY

"We lose out on 100% of the shots we don't take." - Wayne Gretzky

I want to toss out a term that many people haven't heard of. If you've ever considered walking up to and starting a conversation with a stranger hoping to get to know them, you likely experienced some degree of "Approach Anxiety."

While it doesn't matter who makes the approach, I consistently saw that men often took the lead role in this. Therefore, I wrote this section from the perspective of the male making the approach. Regardless, there is plenty of good insight for both women and men in this chapter.

To Approach or Not Approach?

You see an attractive lady. She could be in a coffee shop, walking down the street, standing alone at a party, or sitting on a park bench. You want to approach her and say hello, but you don't.

Why Not?

Because before you moved, your mind ran through the "what if's?" You paused to decide if it's the right timing, the right move, or the right thing to say, and it's already too late. You've already talked yourself out of it.

Sometimes you talk yourself out of it once, and that's it. Other times you say to yourself "It's too awkward here, but if she goes to sit down, I'll do it then. But then she sits too close to other people, so you pause again. All evening it's a series of "maybe's, if's" and excuses. At the end of the night, you never made the move, and you head home beating yourself up over those "what if's?"

Trembling hands, a shaky voice, feeling anxious, sweating, racing heartbeat. It feels the same as if you were being threatened with bodily harm. But if you think about it, these are just the feeling you get when you try anything new or unfamiliar. So, let's look at what is causing these symptoms, so you can get past them.

The Fear of What If…?

I began photographing weddings early in my career. There is a lot to cover at a wedding, and they can be incredibly stressful. For roughly the first twenty weddings I booked, I was petrified as the date approached. Midweek prior to the wedding day, I would find myself with a tension headache. I chewed antacids like they were candy. The tension and "what if's" would last until the wedding was over.

Somewhere around wedding number twenty, I realized it wasn't even on my mind anymore. I'd become calm in the face of the impending storm. While there are plenty of stressful moments on any wedding day, I was beginning to relax and normalize it. Had they all gone perfectly? Of course not. But I'd learned and grown from those situations, and with that, I'd lost my overwhelming fear.

Approaching others intending to meet them is the same. The only way to get comfortable doing it is to practice it. In the process you will learn what not to do and get better at it.

Everyone is different, but many of you, like me, will begin to feel comfortable by or before your twentieth approach. Regardless, the comfort level will improve if you give it the chance to.

What if I Stumble on My Words?

That is okay. We often think the right words make it all work, but that is not the case. When I first got back out there, I was looking for that perfect, smooth line that no woman could say no to. It didn't work. As I mentioned before, I got turned down by the very first lady I asked out. No matter how many times you do this, you'll never be perfect, or hear "yes" 100 percent of the time. Stop waiting till you've got it all figured out. That'll never happen. What is the key to overcoming approach anxiety? Doing it enough times to allow yourself to see that nobody dies over this (even though you might feel you could).

What if I get Rejected?

If you try this twenty times, you will get rejected. But you will find quickly that you will survive to try again. And most women will be nice about it, (and a bit flattered) even if they aren't interested. We make it out to be much worse in our own heads. We must retrain our brain into realizing this. The only way to do that is to practice it.

What if She Has a Boyfriend?

Tell her it was nice to meet her, thank her for her time, and go on.

What if I'm Rejected, and Everyone Hears?

What if everyone sees me get up and walk over? They will all stop to hear her laugh, and say, "No way, get lost". We all have had that little movie playing in our head at some point. Has it ever happened? Yes, but it's not likely. Even if it does, you will live through it.

Am I Overthinking It?

Yes! But you aren't alone. Overthinking it is for most people the single biggest hurdle. Once you allow yourself the time to ponder it, it's too late. It is far too easy to talk yourself out of approaching, because you know you are playing the odds every time you do.

Putting a Stop to Approach Anxiety

Know You Will Get Rejected

This one was hard for me. I didn't even want to think of approaching anyone unless I was sure it would go positively. To get past this, you must consciously shift your perspective to recognize that rejection is normal and moving forward anyway is a big breakthrough. Everyone gets turned down. The only way to avoid getting rejected is to never ask. By the time you've approached and asked others out twenty times, you will have gotten turned down plenty.

If you are taking action and asking, you are already going above and beyond the norm. You will get exponentially more dates by asking than you will by not. Once your adrenaline is pumping, you are more likely to take the same risk again and ask someone else out.

Always Look Your Best

I caught myself too many times in the past just running out to the supermarket to grab one item, and seeing someone, but not approaching because I hadn't showered or gotten reasonably dressed before running out.

As noted earlier in the Acting, Thinking, and Feeling Confident Chapter, always go out looking your best. It'll come back to bite you if you don't. Looking your best makes you feel so much more confident, and far more likely to make the approach.

Start with Hello

Place importance on being more sociable in everyday life, which makes everything else so much easier. If you take the time to speak to people in public situations, you will stand out from the rest of the world. Most people say nothing to others around them in line, in the coffee shop, and on the bus.

Don't wait to speak. If you find yourself in a position to meet someone, yet you stand in silence for some time, it is much harder to strike up a conversation. The first words don't have to be hello. Sometimes it's better to comment on something else, and lead into a hello. Maybe you can comment on the weather, or the smell of the coffee in the shop you just walked into. The surroundings can often provide great context for the small talk you choose.

The words themselves are not nearly as important as the fact that you said anything at all, and that you said it with a warm, confident smile. Those around you immediately sense that you are friendly, and confident.

Make small talk with the cashiers. People are taking notice of you because you are standing out from the rest. When you approach someone you already spoke to earlier it is much easier to engage in conversation.

Be sociable with everyone, men and women. When you are being sociable, people's guard goes down. Don't go into it with an agenda. If you have a goal to get to, that's all your focus is on. If you are just starting the conversation and letting it flow, it's not at all unusual to have her pickup and continue the conversation. This makes everything easier. Any small talk works to continue the conversation, and this is where those questions you committed to memory really come into play.

Three Seconds to Make it Happen

Make use of the three-second rule. It is similar to the rule that allows you to pick up a cookie you've dropped on the floor and eat it anyway. But that rule gives you seven extra seconds, and that's too many.

The three-second rule reminds you to move forward to start a conversation in the first three seconds you see the person of interest. If you follow this rule of engagement, you will not have time to consider whether it's the best thing to do, the right time, if she has a boyfriend, or anything else that'll otherwise keep you from meeting her.

The three-second rule will help keep you from thinking, as that's always what gets you into trouble in the approach. Anytime you find you didn't speak when you wanted to, evaluate why. Almost for sure, it's because you allowed yourself to think about it.

Show Confidence

Women like a guy with confidence (apparent or real). When you use the tools discussed in the confidence section of this book, you will not only appear more confident, you will begin to feel more confident. That's not to say that you will go out and try this your first time and feel completely confident. What it does mean is that it will increase your level of confidence from what it would have been otherwise. Appearing confident as you approach is half the battle.

I enjoy watching rock band documentaries. One thing I've taken away from them is that most musicians get an adrenaline rush from playing in front of a crowd, even after years of doing it. Often, they will comment that they always get nervous before going onstage, never completely getting over that feeling. So, if you feel like a fake for portraying confidence, you aren't. It means you are normal.

Approaching with a smile and looking that other person in the eye as you strike up a conversation gives an incredible illusion of confidence. With practice, it only gets easier.

Turn the Tables

As you approach someone you have an interest in getting to know, it's common to think, "I sure hope they like me." Switch your own perspective on this, and approach with the question "I wonder if I will like them." It's a simple but profound turn of the tables that empowers you.

Keep it Positive

There are plenty of reasons you could get rejected. Realize this and have fun anyway. If the answer is "No," smile and thank her, and leave the situation on a positive note. You will be glad you did, and it'll put you in a place that you can pick up and move on from quickly. If you leave it in a negative state, it'll affect both your mood and your perspective for a much longer time.

What can Women Learn from This?

Realizing that Approach Anxiety exists may help you recognize what is likely going on in a guy's head who may be interested in you. In many cases, you can place yourself in scenarios that directly increase his likelihood of coming over to meet you, if you choose not to make the approach yourself.

Men are far less likely to approach you if you are in a group of people. Most guys would prefer to approach you individually. The same applies even if it is just you and another female friend or two. If you are with a group, and you spot someone you may have an interest in, break away from your group from time to time, and position yourself far enough from them (or close enough to him) to allow a conversation to start. Or say "hello" yourself.

You may say "I don't want a guy who doesn't have the confidence to approach me". But you may be single-handedly leaving off the greatest guy you could ever meet because he hasn't yet gained that confidence. And he'll gain that confidence with someone else instead of with you. Just a little something to think about.

Closing Thoughts for Men

- When you decide not to approach, you are potentially letting two people down; you and the person you could have met that day.
- Approach anxiety is a mind-game. 95 percent of what's going on is between your ears. The way I overcame it was by getting enough practice to allow it to become easy.
- Approach Anxiety leaves you over evaluating your every move, as if

you had your finger on the button to launch a nuclear warhead. While you are overthinking it, you are missing out on a world of people who want to meet you.

CHAPTER 22
GETTING TURNED DOWN

"Your value doesn't decrease based on someone's inability to see your worth."
- Ted Rueben

Early on, I met Erin online, and drove an hour to meet her in Richmond, VA. She had insisted on the phone she wanted to keep the meeting brief. Once we got there, what I expected to be brief was anything but. We ended up spending hours in deep conversation about her and her son, and I chimed in to answer the questions she asked about me. All seemed to be going very well. The time we spent together after she had insisted this would be a brief meeting made me feel good about the possibilities.

When we finally wrapped things up, I asked her if I could drive down and meet her again soon. It shocked me when she said she didn't have any interest in seeing me again. She used those very words too!

It would have been so easy to let my emotions hijack me each time I got rejected, and at first it did. It's like a hot stove; once you get burned, you don't want to do it again. As you know, rejection isn't exclusive to the dating world. If you listen to the stories of some of the world's most talented people, you will repeatedly hear how they each experienced rejection in attempting to get a career off the ground.

Just as important are the stories of happy individuals in your everyday life that got past the fear of asking the man or lady out that they are married to. This isn't just your fear. We all experience it at times.

Concerns about rejection aren't held solely by the person asking someone out either. You can fear rejection in many forms, including going out but never being approached. That feeling is a lot like that of the last kid on the playground who hasn't gotten picked to be on a team yet (which was me as well).

I was acutely aware that if I If I didn't allow myself to get back into the dating game, I could avoid all the discomfort of rejection. But I was just as aware this would keep me from experiencing the possibility of love and partnership that I was seeking.

What's Really Behind the Feeling We all Hate?

The most interesting thing about rejection is where it originates. We always think of rejection as something done to us by another person. Rejection is less about what the person says to you, and more about what you say to yourself when they stop talking. When they stop, the voice in your head starts. And when it talks, it's telling you all the negative things you already feel about yourself. It's our own "critical voice" afterward that brings on the hurt and emotion.

Breaking it Down

Let's dive a little deeper into rejection and consider how understanding the source can unravel some fears that can prevent you from trying again.

If I walk up to you and say, "You have the ugliest mohawk I have ever seen," would that offend you or make you feel rejected in any way? You might think I was nuts if you did not have a mohawk and I said that to you. You might look behind you to see if I'm talking to someone else, but you wouldn't likely be offended. Why? Because unless you have a mohawk, you know this isn't a factual statement.

We've all had a situation where someone reacted rudely to us, and we knew we were innocent, and while we might have gotten mad, we knew they were wrong. But the key thing was, we didn't sense rejection from it.

What happens, however, if you are sensitive about your weight, and someone makes a comment about your size. That's where the conversation stops on the outside, and picks up on the inside, because you've felt this way already, and now you are hurt by that statement.

In my case, the fear of rejection when asking a lady out, I had an imagined experience of being turned down because I wasn't a good catch. That fear of rejection would start the conversation going in my head. The doubt about me already existed. Being turned down (and even imagining it) starts that internal conversation. So, the next time someone makes a statement that creates a feeling of rejection, remind yourself that it's what you say to yourself when the conversation stops that really brings out the emotion.

The more another person of interest appears to meet our needs, the more value we mentally place on that person. This can include both their physical attractiveness and other highly regarded qualities we see in them. When I would meet an attractive lady, for example, my concern of rejection would go up exponentially. Subconsciously, I would place a greater value on that person's opinion of me, because I felt like there was more at stake, and that I was less likely to hold enough value.

This doesn't have to all about looks either. Any characteristic that heightens your interest in another person raises the bar. The need for acceptance and approval increases in direct proportion to the attractiveness and characteristics you find important. Therefore, the more attractive that person's characteristics are to you, the greater the concern of rejection.

This sets me up to be in a position of need, however, while they hold the position of power (without even knowing it). The key to confidence in this scenario is that you feel attractive and valuable yourself. As said before, when you feel good about who you are, others will more naturally feel good about you. It is amazing, but it's true.

The Deeper Effects

When you are down on yourself, it is common to respond to rejection with what therapists would call a global belief…" No one wants me" or "Who would ever want me?" It becomes bigger than just that one rejection and turns to "I'm really not good enough for anyone." When I can recognize that I am of value to God, and the world around me, I can better handle the rejection. I can see it as a single event, as opposed to how valuable I am. When I turn it into a belief that "No one would want me," I am more likely to erect walls of protection to shield myself from future hurt.

Have you ever been in your yard, and encountered a snake? What happened the next time you went back to that same area of the yard? Did the snake cross your mind? Did you look more cautiously, or avoid the area altogether? The likelihood of that snake being at that same spot in the yard again was minimal. Yet every time you went back there, that snake crossed your mind, and it affected how you acted or reacted.

The same can be true of dating. You go out with someone you met on an online dating site, and it didn't go well. Do you know how many people have told me they won't use online dating because of a bad experience? Every time they even think of going back, their minds go back to those anxious experiences. These experiences created such negative reactions that they avoid that side of the yard because they are sure they will see the snake again.

This self-protection mode is obviously helpful in allowing you to learn from past experiences. It can also envelope you in fear, keeping you from trying again, after a bad first experience.

Here is What We Learned About Rejection so Far:

- It is a common fear all of us deal with at some level.
- Rejection is the same in the business and social world.
- None of us like it.
- We tend to avoid it, like most things we don't like.
- It is based on how we feel about ourselves.
- The greater the "value" we place on the other person, the greater the fear and the sting.
- When I go in hoping they will like me, I place myself in a position of need, while the other person holds all the power.
- My own critical voice begins talking when the other person stops.
- It's what I say to myself when the conversation stops that brings out the emotion.

Putting a Stop to the Sting

Recognizing that the strong feelings associated with rejection are grounded in your own feelings about yourself is often a breakthrough. But there are additional ways to combat the reaction your mind and body have to rejection.

I mentioned the Thought Stopping technique earlier, where you yell "Stop!" to when you find that you are beating yourself up. You should do this silently, of course. No one else needs to hear this, or they will wonder about you. You can use this at the moment of rejection, or anytime you put yourself down.

This technique allowed me to cut off my own critical conversation anytime I caught myself. Then I would fill in the void with something positive. This rebuttal will be your counterattack to short-circuit your own critical conversation. Referring to the positives list we made earlier in the book may help you with building a rebuttal.

A positive Statement Such As:

- "I have a lot to offer, and this won't stop me."
- "It's their loss."
- "They really don't know me well."
- "I really didn't like you anyway."
- "This didn't work, so God obviously has someone better for me yet."
- "This just means I didn't waste any of my time on them."
- Use one of these or create your own.

Again, these aren't for stating out loud, but for reminding yourself that these are temporary setbacks that don't have the power to get you off course in this journey.

I needed to have those statements ready in advance, because I wanted to stay in control of my response when those scenarios occurred. This takes practice, and a predetermined rebuttal. Trust me, without a rebuttal, you will spend that time beating yourself up.

Just being aware of what creates the pain of rejection in your own heads is a help in better understanding yourself, and the Stop technique gives you a way to fight back in your own head, instead of letting the negativity take control.

You may have hoped that with this book would give you the tools to never get rejected. In truth, you will likely get turned down more because you will put yourself out there more than ever. That's a good thing to understand and realize that you can bounce back from. It's the bounce back that'll keep you moving in the right direction.

There are as many reasons to get rejected as there are ants at a picnic, and most don't have to do with our looks. It took me a while to realize I can't be all things to all people, nor do I want to be.

Some Reasons You Might get Rejected:

- That person isn't at a place in their life that they have an interest in meeting anyone.
- That person just got in a fight with their boss, mother, child, best friend, etc.
- The person is shy and panicked when approached.
- The person isn't interested in you based on something that has

nothing to do with what you are sure you got rejected for.

There are so many reasons someone could turn you down that it would be impossible to list. But your mind always goes to whatever you see as your shortcoming.

Reasons I can Remember Getting Turned Down:

- I wasn't tall enough.
- My work didn't leave me free every weekend.
- I go to church.
- I had too much energy.
- I wasn't exciting enough.
- I didn't make enough money.
- My career wasn't the kind they were interested in (in other words I didn't make enough money).
- I had a dog.
- I have children.
- I spent too much time with my kids.
- I wasn't interesting enough.
- I wasn't Catholic.
- I don't drink alcohol.
- I wasn't willing to relocate.
- I lived too far away to date.
- I don't have a college degree.
- I didn't "man up" and tell my date where we were going to eat. Instead, I asked what she liked. But she wanted to be told where we were going, which was not my style.
- I might be a serial killer because I had a pair of scissors in my vehicle glove compartment.

I'm sure there were others, but that is a quick list I compiled to show you aren't alone. What did I believe every "no" was about? I assumed that it was my looks, or my income. Why? At the time, I believed those were my weaknesses. So, I naturally assumed it was one of those two every time.

I talk to people every day who blame their weight, knee replacement, looks, job, health or economic status for their lack of ability to find someone who will love them. I was far from perfect, but to the right person, I would be the perfect match. I just had to find that person.

Facing Rejection Head On

How did I deal with rejection? I realized that I had no choice but to accept that it comes with the territory. It's part of the process. If you are putting yourself out there, you will feel rejection's sting.

First, if someone isn't interested in you, don't get upset at them. Just thank them for their time and move on. It truly is the best thing they can do for you. Yes, it hurts, but the way you handle it shows a lot about your confidence, who you are as a person, and just how strong you can be. Many people have stated that when they politely turned a suitor down online, the other person laid out a verbal bashing. This is not how a confident person handles a situation like this, and it's not how you will either.

I heard Rachel Herron, a writing podcaster once talk about the way she and her writer friends approach rejection. As a writer, your work is subject to being reviewed by people all the time. Putting your best work out there doesn't stop the negative reviewers.

The question was raised on how she dealt with the sense of rejection from poor book reviews on Amazon. Rachel mentioned that she and some of her author friends connect with one another to make light of which one has the worst one-star review on Amazon for that given month. They've made a game out of what would have felt crushing before.

These authors aren't hoping for poor reviews. Quite the opposite. But they took something that bothered them at their core and turned it on its head. Sure, the rejection hurt, but I love that idea of making the best of it, and even finding fun in it, which is exactly what they did. The shift in perspective changes everything!

Face it head-on and find some humor in it. On a similar note, I've heard of guys that made a game of it by purposely trying to get turned down. Doing so helped them get used to hearing "no" until the fear of that word dissipated. You could try this yourself, or at the least share your stories with other single friends you meet in this journey. This really is all about your perspective. If you can allow yourself to get past seeing rejection as a traumatic event, and even find the humor in it, it can change your perspective entirely.

Rejection happens to us all. Don't let it stop you. It is at these times that you must remind yourself of "What's positive about this?" If you don't, you can easily get worn down.

The choice to get back up and keep moving forward after rejection is the key element to success. That ability will ultimately be what makes this successful or not.

Getting to the place where I was no longer afraid of the word "no" was incredibly liberating. It allowed me to come from a place of confidence, as opposed to one where the rejector held all the power.

Until that point, my biggest fear was hearing the word "No." It's not "Is this person a good match?" or anything else of actual importance. It was all about my fear of hearing the word "No."

A Twist

I opened this chapter with the story about Erin, who had rejected my offer to meet again. Years later, when I was dating my future wife, Erin sent me a text out of the blue, and wanted to know if we could go out again. I was kind but reminded her gently that she had no interest in a second meeting way back then. She claimed she couldn't recall stating that, but that she just wasn't ready at the time. I wished her nothing but the best, but kindly told her I was no longer single.

At the time Erin had turned me down, I'd wondered what was wrong with me. Don't we all do that? Looking back, I realize that this is a process for every single person who is out there dating. She was not ready at the time, and likely was just beginning to test the waters with me.

Getting rejected will happen, and you rarely will ever know the why. Don't make it about the why. Instead, recognize that it is part of the journey that will lead you to finding the right one.

CHAPTER 23
SINGLE PEOPLE ARE EVERYWHERE

"The greater danger is not that our hopes are too high, and we fail to reach them. It's that they are too low, and we do." - Michelangelo

So far, we've discussed connecting with others through blind dates, online dating services and Meetup Groups. They build relationships with others that can expand your world and give you broader reach. They help provide a rock-solid foundation to expand your social network and fill empty spots in your calendar. These also give you a consistent "go to" source. But they are only the tip of the iceberg.

I talked earlier about going up 10,000 feet and looking down over the landscape. If your pilot could then point out all the single people, you would be amazed at the number of singles so close that you are completely unaware of. Of these, only a small percentage are currently on a dating site or signed up to attend a Meetup group. It would amaze you to know the number you pass in your everyday life. Unfortunately, they aren't wearing a shirt that says, "I'm single."

I've saved this option for last, because for most of us, meeting others in public situations and striking up conversations from scratch is the most difficult. Yet all that you've learned up till now has given you the tools you need to do just that. Building confidence in yourself and gaining practice through repetition have already made it easier to open the doors to meet singles in your everyday life, some of which aren't even actively looking for a partner.

I've been in the company of too many people who have settled for someone less than they'd hoped or given up on looking altogether because their world was far too small. Keep growing your world, and you will be less apt to cut yourself short.

Reaching Out Further

Over the years I have photographed over 1000 engaged couples. I always enjoyed finding how and where they met. I can tell you that the number of ways to meet someone is infinite. There are so many places you could meet others it would be impossible to try them all. Some of these possibilities may sound odd to you, and probably would have sounded that way to the couple as well...until they met. Here are some suggestions that will both stretch your reach and your confidence.

What Would you Consider From this List of Interests?

- **Music:**
  - Festivals
  - Open mic nights
  - Karaoke
  - Meetups
- **Animals:**
  - Zoos
  - Dog parks
  - Downtown events
  - Pet events
  - SPCA
  - Pet-related Meetups
  - Volunteering
- **Art:**
  - Classes
  - Museums
  - Galleries
  - Shows and exhibits
  - Art Meetups
  - Photography exhibits
  - Contests
- **Church/Religion**
  - Adult classes

    - Singles classes
    - Worship services
    - Other religious centers and locations outside your own
- **Fitness**
    - Gym
    - Adult Sports Programs
    - Meetups
- **Business Groups**
    - Chamber of Commerce
    - Networking Groups
    - Toastmasters Meetups
- **Parties/Events**
    - Local Singles Events
    - Speed Dating events
    - Weddings
    - Charity Events
- **Children/Family**
    - Join the PTA *(only if you have kids there)*
    - Single parenting groups
- **Favorite Hobbies**
    - Local Clubs
    - Meetups
- **Reading**
    - Library-sponsored Events
    - Bookstores
    - Book Clubs
- **Sports**
    - Sporting Venues
    - Gym
    - Adult Sports Programs
    - Meetups
- **Tours**
    - Walking
    - Hiking
    - Wine Tasting

  - City Tours
  - Group Travel Tours
  - Meetups for Traveling Singles
- **Local Events**
  - Search Online and in Local Papers
  - Facebook Groups
  - Meetups
  - Street Fairs and Festivals
  - Car Shows
  - Convention/Expo Center events
- **Dancing/Dance Classes**
  - Check Local Dance Schools
  - Meetups
- **Talks/Lectures**
  - Events
  - Seminars Through Colleges/Universities
  - Meetups
- **Trivia Nights and Games**
  - Meetups
  - Local Pubs

Guys, you are missing out if you don't try a dance Meetup! Visit meetup.com. Check your local dance school for a schedule. Many offer a night to just pop in and pay a few bucks for a one-hour lesson. I had a lot of one-on-one conversations with the opposite sex those evenings.

The list of places you could meet someone is endless: bookstores, coffee shops, laundromats, movie theaters, and grocery stores name just a few. I've given you several ideas to run with. They will not all be good for you. Just begin with a few that could take you in the right direction.

CHAPTER 24
CONVERSATION STARTERS

"It is in your moments of decision that your destiny is shaped."
-Tony Robbins

The title of this chapter may have you thinking this sounds like the Icebreakers chapter. But this is different. This is an absolute secret weapon, so work to implement this when possible. This tool gives others a reason to break the ice with you.

Sometimes referred to as a prop, a conversation starter could be an unusual hat, bow tie, bag, a camera slung over your shoulder, your dog, a guitar, or anything else that gives someone a reason to approach and start a conversation with you. People are looking for reasons to connect with others, so these conversation starters are a type of icebreaker that gives the other person a chance to start the conversation. From blue hair to an unusual breed of dog, these conversation starters really work!

I once knew a guy who paid for everything small with $2 bills. That was a conversation starter everywhere when he bought something. It's a simple thing, but you don't see $2 bills every day. It made him unique, and it opened the door to many conversations that the other person always started.

Get Started with These:

A Pet

At events, in public parks, or walking along the street, I started many conversations with women because they had their dog with them. Always ask if it's okay to pet them and let the conversation flow. Everyone's guard is down, and conversation takes off on its own.

The more unusual the pet, the more interest and conversation. I am not suggesting you go out and buy something unusual, but if you have an interesting breed of dog already, let the world know. Regardless, if your pet is friendly, he will draw attention.

A Camera

Throw it over your shoulder, and bring it out for a walk, or to any event. This is an overwhelmingly great way to open conversations, for both men and women. I found many women starting those conversations when I had a camera slung over my shoulder. It worked like a magic wand. It works just as well for a female too. So many people have an interest in photography, this one can keep you talking all evening.

One thing to keep in mind; bringing an expensive item to a party or event means you must keep an eye on it. You don't want either slipping out the back door with someone else while you are away at the food table.

A Book

Books can work nicely as a prop in a coffee shop, or in a park. You look smart, and you will find others may ask you what you are reading. It also gives you a conversation starter to ask someone else what they are reading. You can't keep your head buried in the book the entire time, though. Position yourself so you are turned toward the natural flow of people in the shop. You don't want your back turned to the world!

A Guitar

Do you play music? I found taking my guitar to a place where people were getting together, such as a backyard barbeque was a fantastic icebreaker. This one isn't for the faint of heart, though, because bringing it out will bring all eyes on you. A less conspicuous way is to have people over to your place and have the guitar out in a corner. This'll give others the opportunity to ask if you play, and get the ball rolling organically, without feeling like a show-off.

Be Inventive

Be the person who stands out. I once saw a guy bring a cooler filled with bottled waters on ice in the back of his truck for after the long group hike. It was his first outing with the group, but he created instant rapport and left a positive first impression with everyone.

People are often looking to connect with others, especially when there are shared interests. Sometimes the only thing that keeps a connection from happening is having something to say. These props give conversation starting material with the ability to open more doors than you ever thought possible.

CHAPTER 25
CONTINUING THE CONVERSATION

"The only place success comes before work is in the dictionary."
-Vince Lombardi

Keeping the conversation flowing once it has begun.is an art. When you meet someone new, always offer your name and be prepared to listen. Often people fail to give you their name in exchange. I am always prepared to ask if someone doesn't immediately offer it in the process of the first handshake.

If you forget their name after you ask, don't beat around the bush about it. Just ask again, and repeat it to yourself, or associate it with someone else with that name as a temporary reminder. The great thing is that others are usually also caught up in what to say and aren't listening for your name either. If you ask again, remind them of your name as well.

Use their name at times throughout the evening when possible. People will often be surprised when you remember their name later. It makes them feel important, and you are more memorable for that alone.

When I first got started on this journey, I was so busy thinking of what I would say that I'd forget to listen for their name. When you introduce yourself to someone, listen carefully. Make your introduction short, which frees your brain to listen for their name.

Tips for Getting Their Name

- Approach with learning their name as your number one goal.
- Smile on the approach, and start with something simple like "Hi, I'm ________," as you extend your hand to shake. Often, they will reply with a "hello" and their name.
- The person you are meeting may just say, "Hello" and shake hands without giving their name. If so, ask "What is your name"?
- Armed with that name, use it immediately. "Great to meet you Jim". If I know someone else with that name, I'll mentally record that to help me associate it.
- Don't feel bad if you have to go back later because you've forgotten and ask again. Nearly every person I've ever asked a second time said, "Oh, don't worry, I'm terrible with names." They then ask me for my name again.
- Sometimes it's an unusual name. It's perfectly okay to ask them to repeat it. If it is difficult, they know it. They may laugh, because it happens to them often. They may offer a nickname or shortened version instead.
- You can further remind yourself of their name by repeating it throughout the night when you run back into them, or introduce others to them, using their name. Both further solidify it in your memory.

Later, I would record that name under the title of "People I Need to Remember," in the notes section of my phone with a brief description of where I met them, and any features that would help identify them when I looked back later. Here I would commonly add people I felt likely I would talk to again. This gave me a place to review the new people I met again later.

Because most people have trouble remembering names, when you do remember, that really makes you stand out to them. It sets you apart, which is always a positive.

Let Them Do the Talking

Think for a moment about enjoyable conversations you've had in the past. It likely involved you talking about something of great interest, while the listener showed genuine interest through eye contact, gestures, comments & questions. Whether you gave advice, told a story, or had an otherwise engaging conversation, you spoke of things you had a passion about, and felt connected by the other person's interest.

By starting conversations that allow others to talk about their interests, give advice, and share stories of their lives, you create conversations that the other person enjoys. Recognize that they will walk away from this feeling you truly listened, and what they had to say seemed important to you. They will also remember that they enjoyed talking with you, even if they did all the talking.

If you are a natural talker, as I am, it can be tough to listen without throwing in your own two cents. If you are not a talker, learning some questions to ask to keep the conversation rolling will keep you from having those awkward moments where you don't know what to say. The questions will allow the other to keep the conversation rolling.

Asking questions will give you the tools to get started either way. A good place to start is to ask questions that allow the other person to reveal their interests. Allowing people to talk will show you their passions and interests quickly. This will allow you to learn more of who they are, while leaving them remembering a great experience with you. Plus, it is typically easier to keep the conversation going without long, awkward pauses when you have questions to ask ahead of time.

It's Hard to Walk Away from a Good Listener

Use questions to keep the conversation alive. Here are just a few;

- Are you originally from here?
- Do you have family in the area?
- What type of work do you do?
- How long have you been in your profession?
- Did you see the game last night?
- Are you a reader? If so, what do you enjoy reading?
- Do you have any pets? (This one is good if you are a pet lover, or allergic!).
- Any upcoming travel plans?
- How do you two know each other?
- What is your favorite time of the year?
- What was your favorite subject in school?

Use Questions Pertinent to the Situation or Location

- What brought you here?

- How do you know the host of the party?
- What is your favorite band?
- What is the best concert you've ever been to?
- What is your favorite movie of all time?
- Do you like the line of work you are in now? If you had the choice to do anything for a living, what would it be?

These are just a few of the myriad of questions you could open a conversation with or use to keep it going. I don't suggest you try to remember all of these, but the more questions you have under your belt, the less you will find yourself in awkward silence. Start by committing three to memory and build from there. As you practice this, you'll find some questions feel more natural for you, and you'll remember those. Then you can add more.

Don't like my questions? Do a little online research and make your own list of five to ten questions you can pull together for your arsenal. It's important to have several to pull from before you get into a situation where you need them.

Be sure the questions cover a range of topics. When you do feel an awkward silence moment, moving to a question on a different subject line will help navigate you back into good conversation. The great thing is, the other person walks away with positive memories about the conversation, instead of an awkward moment where no one knows what to say, which sent you both heading in separate directions. You want to use questions to help guide the conversation and keep it alive.

Be sure not to probe too deeply at first. Probing and personal questions can make the other person uncomfortable. Keep your questions on the light side at the start. For many, the first conversation will hold to topics on the light side but may reveal a hidden interest or two which can often carry the conversation to a deeper level organically.

Allow Your Personal Side to Show Through

Reveal something funny, or sincere about yourself. Revealing yourself on a personal level may seem risky, but it breaks down barriers quickly. When you share, they get to see a deeper side of you. It's best to keep it clean and keep it in context with the direction the conversation was heading already.

Stories out of left field that don't pertain to anything relevant can seem odd, even if you think they are funny. Keep stories in line with your current conversation. Skip any urge to speak badly of past relationships. It never looks good on you, so don't go there. Having several stories in reserve can help when the appropriate opportunities arise to tell them.

Two Approaches to Avoiding the Awkward Silence

Everyone hates an awkward silence. It is common for introverts to avoid conversations altogether for the fear of hitting the awkward silence wall. Having a game plan can help keep you from getting stuck there as often. Here are two methods I use to avoid it. I have used both many times and they work equally well for business and casual acquaintances.

Plenty of Questions Method

This option entails the previously discussed method of having several questions memorized. These questions can help you when the conversation hits a wall. Having several questions to ask in your memory reserve will really help keep the conversation flowing, and questions allow them to talk about their favorite subject; themselves!

Over time, you can build up the number of questions you have committed to memory. Having a few questions up your sleeve when the awkward moments come will help solidify your confidence in reaching out to meet new people.

Drive by Method

Another approach, quite the opposite of the first, is one I prefer for first introductions. When you swoop in for the meeting, have a plan just to stay long enough for the meet & greet, along with a question or two at most. You then excuse yourself, having not hung around long enough to hit "the awkward silence". It allows you to come and go on a very positive note. It also leaves the person you met feeling both positive about you, along with a bit of intrigue. This is quite the opposite of the feeling you get if you run out of things to talk about. Then, in passing, stop back in to chat more, having reloaded with questions. This leaves you in control of the situation and is likely to leave the other person curious about you.

At the point when you return, you've learned a bit about this new person, have had a moment to regroup your thoughts, and possibly gathered a few questions from your notes. You can then stick around for a bit and converse or continue to pop in and out.

Continuing the Conversation: an Overview

- Smile (It's worth repeating!)
- Use the other person's name. It makes them feel important and will make it less likely you will forget it.
- Practice every chance you get at reaching out to people. The more you practice, the more comfortable you become, allowing the mechanics of connection to become second nature.
- A warm handshake or two-handed handshake held for just an instant longer than you first feel comfortable with.
- Be sure to make them feel at ease. You will find this simple act will take the focus off yourself, and because they hold the focus, you will feel less nervous.
- Don't monopolize the conversation. Often, this comes from being afraid of having nothing to talk about or fearing awkward silences. Have a mental list of questions that you can use as needed.
- Be sure you are listening over 50 percent of the time. Be sure to listen, instead of using the time they are talking to think of the next thing to say.
- Asking questions allows the other person to talk. Not only does this make them feel important, it also keeps you from constantly having to find things to talk about.
- Watch for clues of what is of interest to them. The things they show interest in can be a great takeoff point for learning and conversation.
- If it seems impossibly hard for you to remember questions, think instead of topics...music, work, hobbies, vacations, reading, origins, etc., and form questions from the topics.
- Be enthusiastic in your conversation.
- Get in the habit of asking open-ended questions. Questions that can be answered with a "yes" or "no" answer bring the conversation to a dead end.
- Be an active listener. Nod your head if you agree. Smile or show concern when appropriate. Comments such as "uh huh, oh", and "yes" tell the speaker you are paying attention.

- Maintain eye contact. This is another gesture that shows you are listening. Don't let your eyes wander around the room as other distractions try to grab your attention.
- Ask the questions a great detective would ask "Who?", "What?" "When?", "Where," Why?" and "How?" These keep the other person talking, allowing them to feel like a star.

I first recognized the power of active listening when one of my friends spoke highly of another friend, stating "When I talk to Dave, I always feel like what I have to say is important to him". This showed me how important this friend felt when she talked to Dave. Active listening made her feel like she was being heard, and that her conversation was of interest. Do you make others feel like their conversation is important?

CHAPTER 26
GET OUT THERE AND DANCE!

"Do the thing you fear, and the death of fear is certain." -Ralph Waldo Emerson

Dancing was a fear of mine. It is more accurate to say, "Looking like a complete goof on the dance floor" was my real fear. But I had witnessed first-hand from several Meetup events held at parties, wineries, and concerts that those who danced were meeting far more people than I was.

One of the guys in the singles Meetup group knew how to dance. What I noticed was that many of the ladies in our group enjoyed dancing. This guy wasn't any better looking than any of the rest of us, but he was the only one on the dance floor. Dancing gave him a great way of meeting and spending time with the women in the group. He was getting to know the ladies while the rest of us watched from our seats.

Before this realization, I had no intention of getting out on the dance floor. Now that I'd witnessed it, however, I knew I wanted to try it out. But even the thought of it had me breaking out in a cold sweat. Since I don't drink, I didn't have any help from liquid encouragement either.

I had confided in my friend Carolyn that "I don't dance," and she replied, "I'll be sure to get you out on the dance floor." I knew it was time to once again step out of my comfort zone. I was moving from the statement "I don't dance!" to "I'm afraid to dance," which is a shift in perspective. At least now I was willing to entertain the possibility of trying.

She did just what she said getting me out there on the dance floor at a party. I was terrified of looking foolish. But the fear was much worse than the actual doing (it usually is). I quickly realized no one else paid any attention. My heart didn't stop. The sky didn't fall. Though I didn't pull off any Saturday Night Fever moves, no one seemed to care or notice that I didn't know what I was doing. Once this perspective shift occurred, my question became "What was I so worried about all that time?"

Notice that the title of this chapter is not "Learn to Dance," although it never hurts! If you want to get some formal training, many dance schools offer classes on a specific night that you can just pop in on, at any level. I have found groups on Meetup as well for this, so don't overlook that as a source either. This is good for anyone, but for guys, this is a total winner! I attended some ballroom classes and line dancing classes as well at our local dance school. Both were great ways to meet other people in a full-contact sport!

The last dance class I attended was on a snowy Tuesday night in January. The ratio of female to male was 14:1, and I was the one! Tell me another place you can go with a ratio like that. Oh, and I was terrible at it. But the ladies enjoyed that I could laugh at myself while trying it. I was always two steps behind, and none of the moves ever seemed to sink in. But I had a lot of one-on-one conversations with the opposite sex that evening. It was another step in building my confidence.

What to Remember:

- Everybody just expects you can dance unless you tell them you can't.
- Most of us that fear dancing because we don't want to look silly on the dance floor and subconsciously see the room bursting out in laughter at our moves. Realistically, that will not happen.
- The first step is just to do it. Don't think about it for weeks or plan it too much. In fact, it's best if you put yourself in a situation where you will have the chance to dance, and then go for it.
- The first five minutes will be the worst, and you will be sure everyone is watching you. They won't be. People are too tied up in their own concerns about how they look on the dance floor to give even one second of thought to how you look.
- Get out there and own it!

CHAPTER 27
ASKING AND BEING ASKED OUT

"You can't start the next chapter of your life by re-reading the last one."
- Unknown

In previous chapters we have discussed how to meet others, along with the tools to rocket your social life forward. At this point you should be naturally falling into dating.

It is okay to learn your skills asking out people who may not be "love of your life" but are interesting enough to spend a bit of time getting to know better. Honing your skills in less than critical situations is a great way to get started. It lets you work through the jitters, which will be invaluable when you meet someone who really excites you. You may also be pleasantly surprised by going out with someone you might not have otherwise. I often talk to happily married people who say their spouse would not have been their first choice in a line-up.

When you meet someone, and you are ready to ask. "What do I say?" This is the age-old question that many get stuck on. There are no magic words. Stop looking for magic lines, and approach with a short question. Asking "Would you like to go out for coffee?" really is enough.

One slight twist on this for women who are concerned about not wanting to ask a guy out. If the two of you have stalled, and you seem to be moving nowhere fast, you can state "We should go out for coffee". You didn't ask them outright. You did, however, make a statement. If you still don't get an actual date on the calendar from that one, he's not interested, and you can stop wasting time with him.

It's really not about the words. If she is going to say no, she will say no, regardless of how smoothly your words flow forth. He will say yes if he is interested, even if you fumble over your words. Just make it short and ask. The longer you ponder what to say, how to deliver it, and the perfect timing, the more likely you are to say nothing at all.

Before you ask, have a place in mind to suggest. Guys, don't ask her out, and then ask her where she wants to go. Having it thought out makes it feel like you've got plans handled, and that shows confidence. I didn't do this at first, and I learned the hard way that it's always better to have a plan.

With practice, you will relax, and your more confident self will show through. This self-assurance help will you attract people you may not have met otherwise.

This really is a numbers game, and you typically need to date many people to find the right one for you. When put it in the right perspective, view each date that doesn't work out as a steppingstone to finding the right one. It's a helpful and smart way to look at it. Later, when you've found that special someone, you will look at your journey, and see that the other dates were part of the process. Always remember that along the way you are building competence, which continues to strengthen your belief that you can do this!

I know a guy who asked a girl out by telling her he had a coupon for Arby's and asking her if she wanted to go. She said yes, and they later got married. While I don't suggest you use this as your pickup line, it helps prove my point that the action of asking is more important than the eloquence of the question. No one knows how many great dates have been missed by not asking. Don't be one of them.

CHAPTER 28
WHY MEET FOR COFFEE?

"The most common way people give up their power is by thinking they don't have any."
- Alice Walker

It is quite common for me to talk to singles who are so anxious about first dates that they avoid having them altogether. But you can't have second dates without first dates, so it's critical to get past. While many would argue with me that meeting for coffee is no first date at all (and I'm not arguing), meeting for coffee or a sweet treat gets the ball rolling for two people without many of the negatives of a traditional first date.

A note here-It doesn't matter if you like coffee or not. I don't drink coffee myself. It's not about the drink. Besides, nearly all coffee shops have an assortment of non-coffee drinks. Many times, I'd ask a lady out for coffee, and she'd say, "I don't drink coffee," to which I'd laughingly reply, "Neither do I!" Meeting for coffee allows you to make it short if you deem yourselves incompatible.

Why Meet for Coffee?

1) It is a Public Location. Most women will have concerns about meeting anywhere that isn't a public place, especially if you met online. If he suggests meeting anywhere that isn't comfortable for you, suggest that it will be best to meet over coffee with your busy schedule. If he insists, let him know you prefer a short visit in a well-lit public place. If he has your best interest in mind, he will be concerned with making you comfortable.

2) It allows you to meet for as short or long as you decide to. I've had coffee dates last for ten minutes, and I've had them last for hours. There were those that I was glad were short, and those I could tell she was happy were short.

Other Advantages of Meeting for Coffee:

- It sounds less suspicious than meeting for a few drinks at a bar.
- This can be a good option for a busy professional to fit time into a tight time schedule.
- The coffee meeting nearly eliminates the concern over who pays, as the expense is minimal.
- If you really hit it off, you can leave there, and go somewhere else. If this happens, it's always best to go to another public location, and to drive separately. Remember, you hardly know this person.
- It is an inexpensive way to get to know someone. If you went on two dates a week and paid, it could cost $50-$150 a week. With a coffee date, it is likely to be closer to $25 per week.

We have likely all been out with someone that we knew we had zero interest in within the first two minutes. Ever sit through a three-course dinner with one? The coffee meeting is a great way to find out if dinner and a movie is a good option.

The Coffee Date

It is my opinion that whoever suggested the meeting should offer to pay. It's okay if the other person turns it down, but I think that's the proper way to approach it. Whoever suggested the meeting should arrive early and be waiting for their guest.

Having three to four questions to ask will help get the conversation going. When you ask a question, follow that topic of conversation as long as it naturally flows. When it comes to a standstill, you can go in a different direction with another question.

One thing worth noting is that I didn't share with any dating prospect what I was looking for in another person. I wanted instead to find out if she had the same values and dreams as I did through natural conversation. This way, I wasn't skewing her answers to fit what I was looking for.

Think about it. If you were intrigued by someone you met, and they told you they were completely obsessed with sports, you may skew your true interests to appear to have a deeper interest in sports than you really do. This can happen in any area, including religion, children, lifestyle, etc. I preferred to ask questions that would lead to answers, and then simply listen.

If You are Interested in Getting Together Again

If a coffee meeting goes well, initiate a second meeting before you depart ways. It's not always easy to gauge another person's interest by what they tell you, as many people are concerned with hurting others' feelings. They may feel they are sparing your feelings at that moment, preferring to reply in a positive fashion (or at least a less confronting one) until you all are separated by a cell phone signal.

There will be times when you are left uncertain about how the other person feels about getting back together again. Even if there was an agreement to see each other again, you can connect electronically to let them know again how much you enjoyed their company, and again express your interest in getting back together. The response you get at this point may help to determine their true interest.

Don't let uncertainty keep you from asking about getting together again. The only way to know is to ask.

In dating, there are two people who are each searching for a desired outcome, and those outcomes will often look very different. Most often, your date won't be a match. You will feel like this is a long-term struggle, and then with enough dates, suddenly you are an overnight success! But as you get started, it's important to expect that the vast majority of times your date won't be a good match.

When We Both Don't Feel the Same

There will be times that one of you is interested, but the other sees no attraction. You may find that everyone you are interested in doesn't return that sentiment. There will also be those that show an interest that you wish wouldn't. This just might be the definition of dating! It will feel like you can't make the right connection. That is the way you will feel right up until you strike gold. This is precisely what dating is, and how it feels for everyone who is sincerely seeking a match. It is easy to internalize it though and think there is something wrong with you. There is no way to make dating a successful endeavor, however, without having these misconnections. You can increase your odds by making specific prerequisites that place you in a better position to meet the right type of people. But it is important to recognize this is what dating is, and this is what dating feels like.

Failure is the normal outcome for a typical date. It certainly is the feeling you have as yet another date ends. Yet it is the only way to get where you want to go.

I went on hundreds of dates to find the love of my life. But I did this strategically and found the positives along with ways to keep my spirits high. Keep going, It's worth the ride.

Be Honest if You are Not Interested in Another Meeting

As you are going out more often, there will be plenty of times that you will meet someone, and not have an interest in a second date. It's important that you have a way to manage that before it happens. If you don't want to see this person again, but the subject of another meeting comes up, don't string them along.

Whether the statement is made in person, or via a message later, a statement such as the following is kind and classy, yet leaves no questions about future dates: "I really enjoyed getting to meet you, and I appreciate all the effort you put into this. While I didn't feel the connection, you are a great guy/lady, and I am sure you will make the right person very happy. All the best…"

While It is kind, it does not leave room for negotiation about seeing each other again. This feels terribly hard to do, it is far kinder than leaving someone hanging, sitting by their phone, wondering why you simply disappeared. You aren't wasting any more of their time by leaving them hanging, which allows them to get back on the search without being stalled.

If you've ever been on the other end of a conversation that suddenly went dormant, commonly referred to as ghosting, it is emotional. It leaves you hanging, with absolutely no answers. I feel like the right thing to do is to be gentle, but honest. When the tables are turned, and this happens to you, thank them for being upfront and honest, even though it hurts.

Sometimes the person on the other end will get upset because they feel rejected by your lack of continued interest. If this happens, it is most likely a buildup of frustration from all those other dates that weren't upfront with them. This is less a reflection of you, and more of pent up frustration from past dates that didn't end well. It is important that the statement be kind, yet firm, leaving no wiggle room for negotiations about seeing each other again.

Your choice of words is important, as well as having a statement ready so you don't have to make it up on the fly. A statement such as "I don't think we are a good fit" gives the same result as saying, "I didn't like you," while giving the sense that it's what's best for both of you and without being critical of the other person.

Assessing the Situation

After Your Initial meeting, What Did You Think?

- Did you enjoy this person's demeanor?
- Were any Deal-Breakers exhibited?
- Did their values seem to line up with yours?
- Were any red flags raised from what you'd learned about them?
- Did you feel attracted to your date?

Reaching Out Again

Early on, I found myself concerned with how quickly I should communicate again after our initial meeting. People always told me, "You don't want to seem too anxious." I am often asked, "Should I wait a day or two before reaching back out?" Reaching out shortly after the date ended to state that you had a great time is appropriate for both men or women. Think about it this way. If she is interested in me, then she is hoping that I will call or text her after the date. If she is not interested, it doesn't matter how long I take to get back in touch. She is just not interested.

There seems to be a common concern over whether a woman should play a little "hard to get" at this point. Ladies, if you choose to let him do the pursuing, respond to him in a timely manner if he reaches out to you. You shouldn't play hard to get unless you really are not interested.

What Can I Learn from This?

Regardless of how the date went, there are lots of things you can learn from it. I always tried to give myself credit for being back out there, but also to look honestly at how I could learn from each experience to get better at this.

What Can I Improve On?

- Talk less and listen more?

- Fidget less, so I don't appear nervous?
- Be better prepared with questions to keep the conversation alive?
- Be a more active listener?
- Work on my body language?
- Keep eye contact?
- Stay off my phone?
- Avoid bringing up my ex in conversation?
- Be more positive in my conversations?

This is not about dwelling on your shortcomings, or beating yourself up over how you did this, or said that. Just be aware enough of your own actions to look for ways to improve next time.

CHAPTER 29
THE DATING GAME

"Speed is only useful if you are running in the right direction."- Joel Barker

While it is nice if the first date is a memorable experience, don't get caught in the trap of trying to create an over the top first date. There are plenty of books and blogs out there that can give you great ideas for both simple and elaborate dates. I won't spend time on this topic, as I feel it is less important than the other aspects I cover.

My suggestion is to focus on the person during your date and find things that can help you get to know one another. You want to provide an enjoyable experience, but don't concern yourself with dates that resemble what you see on reality television. The right person will be concerned with getting to know you far more than the lavish experience. Keep in mind, the person who requires an over the top experience to be happy is the same person you must try to please for the next fifty years.

Where Do I Go from Here?

Make your initial date something that allows you to get to know each other better. Going places that give you both time to talk, to learn, and to express your interests should be at the top of your list. Lead with a bit of romance. Spend less time with analytical conversations like work, instead focusing on feelings.

This can be a time to share funny or embarrassing stories. Your goal is to see if you two connect emotionally. Going to an arcade, playing on the swings, or ice skating can bring out a playful, natural bonding, and can lend clues to how well your personalities mesh. If things are going well, keep your ears open for clues for future date options.

For our first "date" after two earlier meetings at a coffee shop, I first took Cynde to a park I had gone to since I was a child. It held fond memories, and I could tell her of the many adventures I had there as a kid as we walked. These stories helped fill the silent moments when I wasn't learning more about her.

Plan three to four questions ahead of time that you can ask on any first date to help determine if he or she is a person you would like to see again. These questions should begin to answer more of your Must-haves and Deal-breakers than the coffee meeting did. You don't want to make this feel like an interrogation process, so don't go in for the kill here. Sprinkle those questions in over the course of your date.

We are human and naturally impatient. I feel these new dating apps have only increased our impatience. We want to get to the end quickly and decide if this person meets all our qualifications. Does he want to have kids? Is she contributing to her 401k plan? Does he meet all my Must-Haves? Does she exhibit any of my Deal-Breakers? We want answers to all these questions before the first date ends. However, the first date is the starting gate, not the finish line. This a place for learning if you enjoy talking to and being with this person. It is not the place to get to the answers to your entire Must-have and Deal-breakers list.

The first date offers the space instead to sit back and become an observer. Ask questions and listen. Use this time to ask lighter questions that open the door for deeper conversation to flow. Look for ways to grow in your knowledge of each other, and to learn more of what excites and drives this other person. You can learn a lot more by strolling through a public park than you might learn through an extravagant dating experience.

If you are not an open person, really concentrate on revealing yourself and your feelings in a way that feels slightly out of your comfort zone. It won't seem odd to them, even if it does to you. Allowing yourself to be vulnerable is a scary thing for many of us, but it can lead to a sharing of emotion that creates a memorable experience.

Expect Many First Dates

Odds are that you will have many first dates before finding someone that really strikes you as being a real long-term candidate, so don't get hung up yet on whether this person is the one. It is unlikely they will be. That may sound pessimistic, but it's realistic. It should not be a surprise when you find out that you are not right for the person you went on a date with.

Going on many first dates is something you should expect in advance, so do not look at it as something you are doing wrong. Do not allow it to get you down, or feel it is a negative reflection of you. When you approach your dating in this way, the weight of the world isn't perched on your shoulders to make each date work.

When you hang your hopes on each date being the one, it is crushing when they turn out not to be. It is far better to go in expecting this other person not to be the one. When you find they aren't who you were searching for, make a clean break so you both can move on and move forward. This isn't a race; it is a slow and steady journey.

Chemistry and Compatibility

We are all interested in finding someone who makes our heart skip a beat. What we refer to as chemistry really is just that; brain chemistry. Chemicals such as testosterone, estrogen, norepinephrine, serotonin and dopamine create these initial feelings of excitement and attraction we all want to experience. I'm not knocking it. We all want it. Chemistry itself doesn't sustain a relationship over the long term, though. Compatibility is far more determining of a long-term happiness, which is our goal.

When you experience chemistry with another person, you need to focus even harder on listening to the exchange of words. When you are attracted, you tend not to hear what is being said, and you can more easily overlook things you wouldn't have otherwise. You don't want to wake up a year from now wishing you had seen all the red flags.

Since chemistry makes us feel good, we tend to chase after it. It is easy to settle into a relationship with someone we feel chemistry with even when compatibility is low. Everyday life becomes hard in these situations, because the compatibility is poor.

When you are considering if this relationship is a good fit, ask yourself "Does this relationship overall feel smooth, or is it a struggle?" A good relationship should feel positive. If it is constant work, compromise, and fighting, it is a sign that you are trying to make something work. If it feels like a struggle now, it will not improve over time.

If it requires so much effort to make it work, it's better to let it go. By letting go, you can allow someone who naturally fits with you to come into the picture. It's a far better investment to meet someone who enjoys you for you, than it is to always be attempting to make it work.

Once You've Met Someone

When you meet someone who you enjoy your time with, and that fits the criteria you laid out in the beginning, I suggest taking your time before you become exclusive in the first couple of months. Rushing into a relationship is nearly always a huge mistake. You may hate being single, and I can fully relate to that feeling. Taking the extra time now to get to know this person will pay off in your long-term happiness, though.

Keep your options open while learning all you can about this new person in your life. Don't take down your profile just yet. Remember to go back and look at your Deal-breakers and Must-haves list for anyone you would even consider becoming exclusive with.

Observe

Get to know them deeply. Don't just experience "highlight moments" with them. Experience the day to day. What happens when things don't go as planned? How does he or she handle adversity? You need to experience both good and bad to see how this potential partner treats you under pressure.

People can disguise character flaws for a period. The longer you experience life with them, the more you will get to see the real person you are getting to know. While many people cannot keep a mask on for that long, some negative personality traits will not appear for a year or more. If there are flaws, you want to see them before you consider "I do."

If you are getting pushed to make it official, it is possible they know they can't keep it contained forever. If they are too anxious about moving quickly, there could be a myriad of reasons and most are not good.

Take it Slow

Do you have a habit of jumping quickly into relationships, falling hook, line, and sinker? If so, this persons' presentation may me stunning, but will it last? Some men with commitment issues come on strong in a relationship. Things will feel like an

unbelievable fit. Everything is wonderful. But just as you fall head over heels, he disappears. Be wary when the relationship moves so fast that it's almost a blur.

We are all on our best behavior initially, and this could last for months.

Unfortunately, some of the worst characters know how to put on the best show. You need to take the time to see who this person really is. Slow down. You won't look back and be sorry you did.

If you are feeling the push to become exclusive, let this person know that you are not ready. If they are serious, they should have no problem with this. Keep giving positive feedback about how you feel things are going. Saying things like, "I have a great time whenever I am with you," is an encouraging statement as you take time to grow in the relationship.

Sex

Sex can easily blur your vision for what is a good relationship or not. It can make any relationship appear better than it really is. Be sure to look deeply at the big picture of what this other person has to offer. Neither good looks nor sex by themselves lead to a great relationship. Step back and make sure neither is leading you astray from your original plan.

CHAPTER 30
WHEN SHOULD WE BECOME EXCLUSIVE?

"Vision without action is a daydream. Action without vision is a nightmare."
- Japanese proverb

After a couple of months of seeing this person, you may decide to become exclusive. Before you do, dig deep into the following.

Is this Going in the Right Direction?

- Have you met each other's family?
- Do you feel the two of you continuing to grow closer?
- Do you both feel the same way?
- Is there continued affection, attentiveness, caring, and genuine kindness between you?
- Do you both embrace who the other person is and accept each other?
- Do either of you feel the need to change the other?
- Do you see any personality issues that raise concern?
- Do you always feel safe with this person?
- Does this person hold the same values as you?
- Can you see a real future with this person you are coming to know?
- Will the things that mean the most to you be realistic with this person in your future?

It is critical to look past all the surface flair, and quietly study the individual's character. Consider the old saying, "Actions speak louder than words." Do their actions consistently line up with what they are telling you?

CHAPTER 31
ARE YOU TALKING ABOUT A FUTURE TOGETHER?

"It's time to start living the life you've imagined."- Henry James

If you haven't already worked through the companion course, it is not too late. Go to www.RediscoverDating.com/course and download your free copy now. It will help you work through the details of the book and take action to change your future!

Once marriage has entered the conversation, I encourage you to get involved with pre-marital counseling, so you can both take a deeper look at the relationship from an outside perspective. The following is an overview to keep you pointed in the proper direction.

The likelihood of divorce in a second marriage is significantly higher than first marriages (45 percent), hovering around 60 percent, with an incredible 73 percent of third marriages ending up in divorce court. This should be enough to make you think more deeply and take extra time before ever considering "I do."

Compatibility vs. Commonality

Compatibility is often mistaken for the things we have in common. If we both like going to concerts, or enjoy watching crime shows on TV, those are things we have in common. These commonalities are good but are not a major factor in long-term happiness.

Compatibility really comes down to how we see life, our personalities, our goals, and how we manage conflict. Do we agree and get along at least

80 percent of the time? If you only agree 50 percent of the time, you are in conflict the remaining 50 percent. That will not sustain a happy relationship, even if there is chemistry. When two people approach everyday life from wildly different viewpoints, they often will find themselves in conflict.

What do we argue about? Money, politics, family, sex, religion, politics, sensitivity to each other's needs, alcohol use, children, and being supportive are just a few topics that spur arguments.

Pay attention to how you two manage conflict. Can you talk through it, or does it turn into a heated fight? What happens when things don't go as expected? Do you support each other, or does it become a blame game?

When these conflicts naturally occur, you will approach them in one of two ways; either as finger pointers, or problem solvers. You will either find fault in the other person or work together to come to common ground supportively.

Those that problem-solve together build depth in their relationship. Those that are blaming each other are chipping away at the foundation of the relationship. Even when they survive, they cannot share a good life together.

A good relationship should not constantly feel like hard work. That doesn't mean things are always happy. If your relationship is difficult prior to the honeymoon phase, though, it is a sign that you are likely in a relationship with the wrong person. Life is hard enough without tying yourself down in a relationship full of conflict.

Common Reasons for Divorce

Let's look at some of the most common reasons for marital issues and divorce. How does your significant other fare when you look at these areas of concern?

Physical, Verbal or Emotional abuse

- If there are any signs, get out now. Don't consider other options.

Lack of Equality

- Are you both on equal terms?
- Is your partner motivated?
- What role do you play in making the relationship work? Do you

only seek to fix the other person, or are you striving to make yourself a better partner as well?

Religious Differences

- Do you have the same faith beliefs? This is an area where family can play a major factor. Family may weigh in heavily in influence that you may not expect.
- Differences in faith will play out in your lives, and the spiritual lives of your children.

Lack of Physical and Emotional Intimacy

- Do you feel that your needs are being met? If they aren't being met now, they won't get met once you are married.
- Does your partner show insight and concern for your needs?
- Do you feel emotionally connected? Looking out for each other's needs, along with acts of thoughtfulness and caring on a regular basis continue to strengthen the bond.
- Making your relationship an intimate one is the responsibility of both parties.

Disagreements About Children and Family

- Does your partner care about your children's best interest?
- Do you have a heart for your partner's children?
- Have you both discussed in-depth whether you will consider having children together?
- Family ties can play a deep role in your relationship as a couple. Will family ties on either side create cracks in your relational foundation?

Dishonesty and Infidelity

- Do you feel deeply that you can trust this person?
- Has this person been dishonest in past relationships?
- Do they earn your trust in the way they handle their life?

The inability to trust someone will come back to bite you in the long run. Consider this aspect long and hard.

Finances

Finances are an area that can cause tremendous stress in a relationship. According to a survey conducted by SunTrust Bank, while 88 percent of married respondents in a group of 2000 couples reported that getting together on finances was a key to a successful marriage, only 51 percent of these couples had the discussion before tying the knot.

Dave Ramsey, creator of Financial Peace University and The Dave Ramsey Radio show, divides us into two categories based on how we approach spending. He calls these financial personalities "Free spirits" and "Nerds." The Nerd wants to keep a detailed spreadsheet of all incoming and outgoing in the budget, while the Free spirit may want to spend without concern. The two often end up married, and the ensuing personality conflicts can cause big problems financially.

Dave isn't suggesting that the two personality types shouldn't be married. He just says you need to work together to get on the same page and build a plan you can both agree on. The best time to do this is before you tie the knot!

Consider the Following:

- Do you think alike when it comes to money?
- Do you have similar goals and game plans for your financial future?
- Are you able to talk about your differences?
- Is one of you well-stocked toward retirement, while the other is heavily in-debt?
- Are there signs of a gambling addiction or inability to control buying impulses?

Be on the same page with a financial plan for your future before you say, "I do." Having this conversation and then planning together can strengthen your bond, prevent future problems, and help build trust and cooperation.

Communication and Disagreements

Everyone grows up with their own communication style. Some people stop communicating and disappear when they are upset or under stress. Others insist on getting the last word. Some become passive-aggressive. Determine to talk about how the two of you can approach your communication differently if it isn't working. A real key is the willingness to consider different approaches, along with agreeing on what is acceptable or not ahead of time.

- Are you happy with your level of communication?
- Is your overall communication positive or negative?
- Do your disagreements turn into shouting matches?
- Every couple argues sometime. But are you arguing constantly about the same things?
- When you argue, are you unable to come to a mutually agreeable resolution?
- Some people must always win any argument. Does this describe your partner? Does it describe you?

I put this one in last for a reason. The key to being able to work out the differences is communication. Can you two communicate about your differences and work to solve them? If you can do this, that's a real positive. If not, I'd suggest you consider the future, and how these concerns could impact or derail your relationship.

Dr. John Gottman and Robert Levenson began studying couples in the 1970s hoping to determine what makes the difference between happy and unhappy couples. The two doctors found that they could predict divorce with over 90 percent accuracy. What was it they found that gave them such a high predictability rate?

Their research showed that for a marriage relationship to thrive, there needs to be a ratio of at least 5:1 of positive correspondence to your spouse for every negative during times of conflict. I know a lot of couples who don't even have a 2:1 ratio of positive correspondence in their day-to-day lives, much less when in conflict.

Is this relationship that you are in a positive one? Do you lift each other up or bring each other down? This is a great way to gauge the overall health of the relationship. The more often kindness is shown in a relationship, the deeper and richer that relationship becomes.

As we wrap up, you now have a system in place that will carry you through the dating process to find the kind of relationship you are seeking. Don't give up and settle for someone just because they are already in the picture. Keep your options open. Don't date exclusively until you've gotten to know this person well and see that they are truly the type of person you are looking for.

Don't write people off too quickly and don't write them off for trivial things that won't make any difference in the long run. You will meet no one who is perfect, but they should meet most of your wants, share the same values, and have zero of your deal-breakers.

What Does a Great Future Look Like?

The Test

You will remember this exercise from early in the book. Five years from today you run into an old friend from high school. The two of you stop for coffee to catch up. You tell your friend you have gotten married. The friend asks, "So, how are things for you?" You reply, "Things have never been better."

Take some time to describe what made you give your mate such a raving review of your life together. How does your partner treat you? How does your partner treat your family? What do you spend free time doing together? How is life better than it was before you met?

Based on all you know now about this person you are dating, is this the scenario that the two of you are creating? Did you have a hard time seeing the person you are dating in this happy scenario? The answers to the last two questions should tell you something. Is it what you want to hear?

CHAPTER 32
THE DAY I MET MY WIFE

"I found the one my heart loves."- Song of Solomon 3:4

As Paul Harvey used to say, "And now, for the rest of the story..."

On a warm summer morning, I met a lady named Kari after an initial connection online. We chatted outside a Starbucks in the sunshine for hours. We had many things in common. She was interested in photography; she was a musician and played music at her church. She had kids roughly the same age as mine. Our conversation came easily, and we laughed a lot that morning. When we finally had to part ways, I told her I would like to do it again. We headed our separate ways after agreeing to meet again soon.

After parting ways, I sent her a message stating how much I enjoyed getting to meet her. She didn't reply for seven hours, and then only with a curt "maybe again sometime." It was a different answer than when we were face-to-face. To say I was disappointed was an understatement. After many such occasions, I could have given up. If I had though, I would have quit just hours short of finding the one I was looking for.

That same day I got disappointed by Kari at Starbucks; I met my wife Cynde at the Hyperion coffee shop. The lady I met on the OkCupid dating website who did not have any photos, and only a few lines in her profile, would eventually become my wife. I am a little biased, but it couldn't have been written better in a movie script.

I couldn't have seen it coming. I didn't. What if I'd thrown in the towel after getting turned down by Kari? What if I had given up that day and said,

"This is too much, I'm done with this?" Cynde and I never would have met. I wonder how many people give up on finding the best partner a day too soon.

I met many people that could have made good partners, but Cynde was the only one with the full array of qualities that I had sought. Looking back, if I had not taken the extra time to find someone with deep compatibility, I could have ended up with a very different life. I made the right choice, and she is worth all the time and effort I put into finding her.

She is everything I could have ever asked for in a wonderful human being. As of this writing, we've been married nearly three years. We have four children between us and are now grandparents. I am truly as happy as I can be, and I think she would say the same.

For me, this journey was a thorough commitment to finding the right person, no matter how long that took. But Cynde's story was far different from mine. I was the first date she went on after her divorce, at the urging of a coworker. She would have never expected these results. Don't set a deadline and expect to find the right person in a set timeline. It differs for each person. For me, it was three years of learning. For her, it was the very first date.

IN CLOSING

Be diligent but seek to find joy in the journey. You can't know ahead how long it will take, or how many frogs you may have to kiss. This book and companion course will continue to expand your world and your perspective if you allow it to. I wish you the best. There is someone out there for you, and I believe you will find that person. Don't give up one day short, my friend.

I wish you only the best in your personal journey. I pray that you too will find the perfect life-partner. Reach out to me at larry@rediscoverdating.com and let me know when you do. I'd love to hear your story.

All the best,

Larry

BIBLIOGRAPHY

1. Center for Disease Control. 2016. Retrieved from https://www.cdc.gov/nchs/fastats/obesity-overweight.htm
Center for Disease Control. 2016. Retrieved from https://www.cdc.gov/nchs/data/hus/2017/053.pdf

2. National Institute of Health. 2014. Retrieved from https://www.niddk.nih.gov › Health Information › Health Statistics

3. CNN Money. Jan 18, 2018. Retrieved from https://money.cnn.com/2018/01/18/pf/lack-of-savings-cover-unexpected-expense/index.html

4. Wikipedia. 2019. Retrieved from https://en.wikipedia.org › wiki › Hypersonic_XLC

5. ABC News. July 22, 2013. Retrieved from https://abcnews.go.com/US/flags-roller-coaster-accident-witness-victim-questioned-secured/story?id=19731762

6. Christakis, Nicholas A. M.D., Ph.D., M.P.H., and James H. Fowler, Ph.D. New England Journal of Medicine. "The Spread of Obesity in a Large Social Network over 32 Years" September 11, 2018. Retrieved from https://www.nejm.org/doi/full/10.1056/NEJMsa066082

7. University of Michigan. "Stop Negative Thoughts: Getting Started." Thought Stopping. Retrieved from https://www.uofmhealth.org/health-library/uf9938

8. Pease, Allan and Barbara Pease. "The Definitive Book of Body Language: Understanding the Basics." The New York Times. Sept 24, 2006. Retrieved from https://www.nytimes.com/2006/09/24/books/chapters/0924-1st-peas.html

9. McKinley-Invrin. Oct 2012. Retrieved from https://www.mckinleyirvin.com/family-law-blog/2012/october/32-shocking-divorce-statistics/

10. SunTrust Bank. Jan 7, 2019. Retrieved from https://www.prnewswire.com/news-releases/get-engaged-over-the-holiday-its-time-to-set-a-dateto-talk-about-money-300773761.html

11. Ramsey, Dave. Retrieved from https://www.daveramsey.com/blog/nerds-and-free-spirits-can-unite-over-the-budget

12. Gottman, John Dr. And Robert Levenson. October 2017. Retrieved from https://www.gottman.com/blog/the-magic-relationship-ratio-according-science/

13. Harvey, Paul. 1977. "The Rest of the Story." ABC Radio Networks. Paul Harvey was an American radio broadcaster for the ABC Radio Networks. He broadcast News and Comment on weekday mornings and mid-days and at noon on Saturdays, as well as his famous "The Rest of the Story" segments.

ABOUT THE AUTHOR

Larry W. Stone is a speaker, coach and consultant on rebuilding confidence and a social life when starting over. A Professional photographer for nearly thirty years, Larry is an optimistic observer of life and the human spirit.

He and his wife Cynde reside in Fredericksburg, Virginia. Together, they have four grown children and two grandchildren (so far).

When he is not writing, speaking or creating photographic images, Larry includes food and music among his many hobbies. Yes, eating really is a hobby of his.

Larry invites you to find out more at:

www.ReDiscoverDating.com.

Want to join in on the conversation? Find him on Facebook at https://www.facebook.com/ReDiscoverDating.

You can also contact Larry directly at larry@ReDiscoverDating.com

www.ingramcontent.com/pod-product-compliance
Ingram Content Group UK Ltd.
Pitfield, Milton Keynes, MK11 3LW, UK
UKHW020424250726
13967UKWH00007B/2800